— GUIDE TO —

SELLING
YOUR
HOME

**EVERYTHING YOU NEED TO KNOW
TO SELL YOUR REAL ESTATE
WITHOUT (OR WITH) A BROKER
IN A COMPETITIVE MARKET**

GUIDE TO
SELLING
YOUR
HOME

ISBN:0-929230-07-8

Author: Brad G. Greer
Contributing Editors:Marcia Castaneda, Charlene Brown
Cover: Vicky L. Andorf
Illustrator: Carolyn Davis

Book Trade Ordering:
Publishers Group West
4065 Hollis
Emeryville, CA 94608
1-800-365-3453
or
Ingram Book Company
347 Reedwood Drive
Nashville, TN 37217-2919
1-615-793-5000

To order a copy for your library:
Quality Books, Inc.
918 Sherwood Drive
Lake Bluff, IL 60044-2204
1-708-295-2010

If and only if, you cannot get the book at your favorite bookstore, you may order by sending address and money order/check for $8.95 ($5.95 + 3.00/shipping and handling). Send to: 4521 Campus, #388, Irvine, CA 92715. No credit cards/no phone orders.

Your best option is your local bookstore or library. Thank you.

PREFACE

The purpose of this book is not to inspire or encourage an overall attitude of anti-realtor or anti-broker, nor to suggest the avoidance of such professionals. The real estate sales industry fulfills an extremely important need in today's society by applying principles, expertise and experience in the marketing of real estate.

The purpose of this book is rather to inspire, motivate, and extend to enthusiastic homeowners the opportunity to gain knowledge and thus possess the sporting chance to market and sell his own home successfully. In turn he will have the ability to save and place back into his bank account literally tens of thousands of dollars of hard-earned, long awaited equity.

This book is being offered as information only and is not intended, in any manner, to replace the need for legal or professional counsel.

DEDICATION

This book is dedicated to all of the millions of men and women in America who once had a dream... of owning their own home, and to all of those who have fulfilled that dream.

TABLE OF CONTENTS

CHAPTER I

GETTING STARTED

Your decision to market and sell your own home was a good one. You have decided to pursue a venture which, when properly guided, can be a very exciting one and extremely gratifying one, and most importantly, will make and save you many thousands of dollars that would have gone to real estate commissions. It's hard to imagine just how quickly the numbers add up.

The most common real estate brokerage commission tends to linger around the neighborhood of 6 percent.

Let's take a look at what this means in dollars:

Sales Price of House	Real Estate Commission
$100,000	$ 6,000
$150,000	$ 9,000
$200,000	$12,000
$250,000	$15,000
$300,000	$18,000
$350,000	$21,000
$400,000	$24,000
$450,000	$27,000
$500,000	$30,000

The numbers do add up very quickly, and it becomes obvious that a good chunk of your hard-earned, long-awaited equity gain will be lost in real estate commissions. Would you pay yourself $10,000, $15,000, or $20,000 to spend a few months and take a little effort to market your home? Would you pay yourself this type of money to work a few hours a week for a few months working with your favorite and most valuable belonging? If you're like most people, the answer will be YES. Most people, however, will never have any idea where to begin with this venture and therefore never do.

Would you pay yourself $10,000, $15,000, or $20,000 to spend a few months and take a little effort to market your home?

So why do so many people let this opportunity pass them by? The answer is simple: The lack of knowledge which in turn inspires and feeds one of the greatest human emotions—fear. Where do I start? How do I get people interested in my home? How do I sell my home? I'm not a salesman. How do I write up a contract? Will I foul it up? What will I do about the escrow? And so on. These are all feelings which are fed by a lack of knowledge and the fear of failure. Remember the old expression, "There is no success without failure, but without failure there is no success at all"?

Everyone at one time or another has been afraid to do something, but when they finally tried and succeeded, they asked themselves why they were afraid. What happened between the initial fear and actual event was that they tried. They gained knowledge through the course of trying.

You now have the chance to learn every aspect of selling your own home step by step. Read this entire book.

So, what does all this have to do with selling your home? Your chances of failing have nearly been eliminated now that you have gained access to the magic doorway with the key to success, that of knowledge.

You now have the chance to learn every aspect of selling your own home step by step. Read this entire book. Let it sink in. Read it again and let the overall concept settle. Make a list of the things you will be needing (a list like this can be found in the appendices of this book) and have them ready as you begin. Develop a positive attitude toward the entire project and maintain this positive attitude throughout. This is extremely important to create and maintain a smooth and easy marketing program. As you begin your venture, read the chapter that relates to the particular phase you are entering. Follow it as you would a textbook. The chapters are conveniently arranged in the same sequence as you will encounter in marketing and selling your home.

The Best Time

For whatever the reason may be, you have decided to sell your home, and you have also decided to sell it yourself. You may be asking, "Is it the best time?" Many variables are involved in the answer to this question. Homes sell throughout the country every month of the year. There are tendencies, however, for typical seasons to evolve which are better for home selling. This means that prices will remain more stable during these peak selling months.

Regardless of the type or size of home you are selling, one last mini-surge will inevitably occur sometime between fall and Christmas.

If you were selling a home which would typically attract families, those families would probably begin looking for a home around March or April with a move-in access around summer. This way the kids would not be changing schools during the school year. This type of surge will last throughout the summer, and will vary in length depending on the climate in that part of the country. Families typically do not like to move during the cold months. They're tucked inside their own homes in front of the fireplace, probably planning for Thanksgiving and Christmas.

If you are selling a home that may appeal more to the single sector, young couples, or retirees—such as a condominium, townhouse, or small house—the surge period may be somewhat different, not necessarily focused around the warm months but more evenly spread out throughout the year. The single professional may have been transferred in January, the young couple may have been married in November and looking for a home. The retirees may have decided to sell and move from their larger home at Christmastime when their grandchildren convinced them their house was too big for their new leisure lifestyle.

The more time you have, the less pressured you may feel, and the better job you will do in maintaining your price.

Regardless of the type or size of home you are selling, one last mini-surge will inevitably occur sometime between fall and Christmas. For those buyers who searched fruitlessly during the summer months to find their dream home, the realization occurs that if they don't become serious, they'll be out for the Christmas holidays. These people can be found rigorously combing the streets searching for their new home wearing the heaviest of winter coats. Their vision is that of a Christmas tree or holiday decor placed into each home they preview.

The bottom line is this: you will be selling only one home... your home. You may or may not have the luxury of deciding exactly when you would like to market your home. The more time you have, the less pressured you may feel, and the better job you will do in maintaining your price. All of the surges and home-selling statistics in the world should not prevent you from selling your home when you feel the time is right.

Pricing Your Home

In general, homeowners tend to stay abreast of the going prices of homes in their neighborhood. Real estate fliers, local newspaper ads, and neighborly conversations all tend to update the homeowner on going prices.

Pick up your local newspaper and start reading through the classified real estate section. Pinpoint homes which are identical to yours, taking special note of upgrades which they may, or may not, have.

You should prepare a market analysis sheet, one may be found in the appendices of this book,

---

Carefully review the real estate fliers which are commonly sent to you in the mail or left at your door. They will usually show both listing prices and selling prices of recent sales. If selling prices were close to listing prices, then the demand for that housing was high, and the selling time was probably short. This difference between listing and selling prices may be applied to (subtracted from) those asking prices which were found in the newspaper classified ad section. You should prepare a market analysis sheet, one may be found in the appendices of this book, which will help you create a comparison between your home and other homes.

One other method of determining the market value of your home is to hire a licensed real estate appraiser. Expect to pay anywhere from $75 to $300 on the average for this service, though if you are in doubt of your home's value it may be money well spent. Your home may be worth considerably more than you had expected. The appraised value that you are quoted would be your selling price, not your asking price, so add a cushion to this value to create your asking price.

Establishing an accurate and reasonable price for your home is very important. If the price of your home is too high, in comparison to other equivalent homes you may reduce its marketability and it will probably take longer to sell. Banks will loan only a certain percentage of your home's market value and this market value will be determined by the bank through their own appraisal. If the price of your home is higher than the bank's appraised value, then a buyer of your home would require more cash to make the purchase. If your home is very unique or has some extremely custom features, then it will demand a higher price. There will be fewer equivalent homes to compare.

If your home is priced too low, then it will probably sell very quickly, but you will be cheating yourself out of your hard-earned cash.

CHAPTER II

CURB APPEAL

One of the single most important factors in marketing your home is, that's right, making it marketable! The term curb appeal is used in the real estate industry to reflect the impression that your home makes from the street, as one first drives up. The old cliche' "the first impression is the lasting impression" applies to your home as well as it does to everything else.

Walk out to the street, turn around, and take a serious look at your house. Do not look at it as you normally would, by anticipating the warm home and comfort that you find inside. Look at your home instead only as a house, from the outside. Look at it as a stranger would look at it. How does it look? How does it compare with your neighbor's house, and the rest of the neighborhood? Does it look better? That's great! Does it look about the same as the rest, or a bit worse? Take a picture of your house if need be and study it. What looks out of place, crooked, or otherwise unkept?

You are offering your house for sale, and you will be competing with other houses for sale, mostly listed by real estate agencies. These other houses will have their

Does your house look like this?

Or does it look like this?
*This house has **curb appeal***

pictures listed in multiple listing books. Your house, however, will have one special advantage. It is being sold by YOU, and whether you believe it or not, YOU will be the most enthusiastic, knowledgeable, and experienced salesperson that your house will ever see! You live and sleep in it every day and who else knows more about it than you?

As other houses are being shown by agencies to customers, there is the tendency toward an impartial viewpoint, on behalf of the agency, toward each house shown. Each house has nearly the same chance of selling until such time that the customer shows a sign of favoritism. You have an edge. You have only one house to sell and you are definitely partial toward its sale. This will be evident in your salesmanship.

You must also carry this edge to include the curb-appeal of your house. If your house stands out from the others, it will not be overlooked. One of your methods of advertising and recruitment of potential buyers will be from people simply driving by. Some people go out for Sunday drives and cruise the neighborhoods. They are looking at homes for sale that interest them and writing down the phone numbers. If your house has curb appeal, it will not be missed. Similarly, you will find real estate salespeople, accompanied by their client (prospective homebuyer) driving through the neighborhoods.

> *...the salesperson, to avoid losing his customer, and though an awkward situation is created, will most likely turn around and assist him with his inquiry.*

They will be most likely searching for a house that they have found in the listing book. If your house stands out from the others, it cannot help but be noticed. If the prospective homebuyer turns his head and shows interest in your house, the salesperson, to avoid losing his customer, and though an awkward situation is created, will most likely turn around and assist him with his inquiry.

What can you do to improve the curb appeal of your house? Think of the answer in the simplest of terms. Think of those items which reflect pride of ownership and suggest a good maintenance history. Lots of money need not be spent.

> *Even if your entire house is in need of paint (and you can't afford to spend the money at this time), it will make a far better first impression if you paint the front door.*

Here are just a few:
(A checklist has been provided for you in the Appendices)
✓Green lawn - make sure your lawn is the greenest in the neighborhood. Visit the local hardware store or garden shop. Invest in a good quality lawn food (to make

your lawn healthy) and ammonia sulfate (to quickly bring out the green).

✓Keep your lawn mowed and edged - more so than normal.

✓Locate and remove all dead or unhealthy-looking plants. If you can't afford to replace them, then leave them out.

✓Add some color. - Invest in a few potted plants and place them by the door step or strategic locations. You can take these with you.

✓Prune and trim all trees and bushes.

✓Broken windows - they must be replaced.

✓Roof shingles or tiles - are any of them mislocated or hanging off the edge of the roof?

✓Mail box - has it been recently painted?

✓Draperies and window blinds - how do they look from the outside? Which position do they look best in? Are they hanging straight?

✓Doorbell - does it work?

✓Front door - access is first gained through this door. Is it clean? If it is in need of paint, then it should be painted. Even if your entire house is in need of paint (and you can't afford to spend the money at this time), it will make a far better first impression if you paint the front door.

The concept of curb appeal also carries its full weight when you own a townhouse or condominium. Remember, it's the first impression that is important. If you live in a condominium and all that is seen from the front is a walkway and a front door, then keep the walkway swept and place a nice potted plant or flowers near the front door. It will display true pride.

Just as there are simple, inexpensive improvements that can be done on the outside of your home, so are there for the inside.

If you live in a townhouse with a small courtyard as its entry, follow the same principles as previously listed. Regardless of size, this is your front yard.

After the front door is opened, you must now create a new first impression. The pride of ownership that was displayed on the outside must be carried on through out the inside. You may not be living in what you consider to be a home decorator's masterpiece. If you are, that's terrific - you will really have the edge. If you are not, then that's OK, too. You will still have the edge. Remember, your goal is to display pride of ownership and evidence of a good maintenance history and not necessarily a decorator's delight. The new owners will inevitably want to add their own decorating to allow the house to feel more like theirs.

Just as there are simple, inexpensive improvements that can be done on the outside of your home, so are there for the inside.

Let's look at a few of these:

✓Carpets - they may or may not be in the best condition, but make sure they are clean. Even a decorator's delight with dirty carpets can be a turnoff.

Place new burner plates under the burners of your stove if applicable. No matter what condition your old ones are in, new ones will always look better. They are inexpensive and found in most super-markets.

✓Walls - must also be clean and free from holes and dents. If need be, use spackling compound for the dents and holes and do a little touch-up painting.

✓Floors - clean and waxed.

✓Kitchen and Bathroom - a key tattletailer to the condition and maintenance background of your home will be found in the kitchen and bathrooms.

✓ Grease and dirt around stove and oven?

✓ Is oven clean inside?

✓ Place new burner plates under the burners of your stove if applicable. No matter what condition your old ones are in, new ones will always look better. They are inexpensive and found in most supermarkets.

✓ Clean grouting between tiles around sinks and bathtubs.

✓ Condition of seal around sinks and bathtubs. Does it need cleaning or repair?

✓ Chipped porcelain in sinks and bathtubs. Repair with a porcelain repair product found in your local hardware store.

✓ Faucets and faucet handles - make sure they're clean and sparkling.

✓ Kitchen and bathroom cabinets - in reasonable order.

✓Burned out light bulbs in fixtures and lamps - replace.

✓Clean windows - makes everything outside look cleaner.

✓Backyard - maintain same as front yard - green cut lawn, trimmed bushes and trees, etc.

✓Pool - if you own a pool, keep it clean and clear. A pool is a large investment and a selling feature of your house. It should look inviting.

» A last note on decorating - if your house is highly decorated, or something close to that decorator's masterpiece, then you have a focal point and a strong marketing tool. Your house will undoubtedly bring in a higher sales price. if your house is not highly decorated, and your plans are to add permanent decor for the soul intent of creating marketability and/or increased sales price, then we recommend the following:

✓ All neutral colors - a dark green or blue carpeting may add a beautiful touch in your eyes, but it will not appeal to the masses. It has long been a general rule that when upgrading a house for resale, always use a neutral theme throughout.

✓ Wallpaper - if using a neutral color, will generally improve marketability but will not increase sales value.

✓ Wood paneling - most wood paneling is of a neutral color and is ideal for masking those hard-to-cover dents in the walls. Avoid dark paneling in dark rooms. Wood paneling will generally increase marketability and sales value.

Avoid upgrades that concentrate a large amount of investment dollars into a small area.

✓ Window coverings - expensive window coverings are beautiful and they will increase marketability but may not necessarily bring back their value in the sales price.

✓ Appliances - if appliances have to be replaced, stay with the middle line of a well-known, quality appliance manufacturer. Spending money for the top-of-the-line appliance may not be the best investment.

If a pattern seems to be evolving, it can be summarized as follows: When investing money in upgrades of a house that is to be sold:

✓ Invest in upgrades that bring you highly visual improvements throughout a large area for a minimal amount of money.

✓ Avoid upgrades that concentrate a large amount of investment dollars into a small area.

CHAPTER III

WRITING YOUR AD

A good number of your leads, or prospective buyers, will come as a direct result of the advertising that you place in the classified ads. Pick up your local city newspaper and also a copy of a county newspaper. Open to the real estate classified ad sections and start reading through some of the ads. Circle those ads that tend to excite you. Look for common links between these ads. What you will probably notice is that these ads all have something very positive to say about the homes they are promoting. The ads that catch your eye are probably not the three or four line ads nor will they be the long, wordy ads.

If the ad is too long, people may not spend the time to read it..

The ads will probably have a large, well-balanced headline that is eye-catching. Look at the illustration. Which looks the most appealing to you, i.e., aesthetically pleasing and balanced? Which ad would catch your eye and cause you to read it?

If the ad is too short, it is very easy to overlook. If the ad is too long, people may not spend the time to read it, or assume that it is either several homes under one ad or simply an advertisement that may not be of interest to them.

Write your ad so that its length is somewhere in the middle—1 to 1-1/4 inches long or around twelve to sixteen lines long. This will be long enough to explain everything that you need to about your home, and short enough not to bore your reader or break your pocketbook. You will probably find that your local city paper will be less expensive to run classified advertising in than your county paper. It's worth a call for a cost per word or special rate estimate. And remember:

—ad too short - you get what you pay for.

—ad just right - best response for the money.

—ad too long - you may receive very little for a lot of money.

Write your ad so that its 1 to 1-1/4 inches long or around twelve to sixteen lines long.

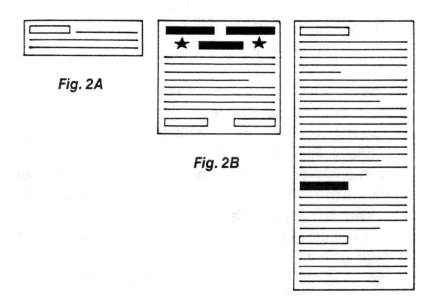

Fig. 2A

Fig. 2B

Fig. 2C.

Take a look at these shapes. Which looks the most pleasing to your eye?

Now, back to the content of your ad. Using sentences that in exclamation points (!) are eye-catching and generally make a very positive statement.

Think about what you liked about your home that caused you to buy it.

Use of such words and phrases as: absolutely, positively, best, finest, spectacular, won't last and rare find all suggest very positively something unique about your property. They tend to stir one's emotions and therefore gain one's interest. Think about what you liked about your home that caused you to buy it. Was it nicely decorated, or did it have a nice view? Is your home nicely situated on a corner lot? Does it have a pool or a large pool- size backyard? Do you have nice landscaping or attractive walkways? Did your home have a quality builder? This list could go forever. Regardless of the type of unique feature your home may have, you must build on that feature, whatever it may be. A few sample ads have been illustrated. Look at ad #3A. Have you noticed what the unique qualities appear to be of this home? The owner feels that:

✓Westview Promenade - (location) is a superior place to live.

✓J.P. Brooks - (builder of house) is a superior builder.

✓Landscaping - unique.

Likewise, in ad #3B, the unique qualities appear to be:

✓"Lakes" condo - (condominium project) is a superior project to live at.

✓"Northern Estates" - (location) is a superior place to live.

✓"unbelievable upgrades" - home is uniquely upgraded.

✓"most spectacular" - home is all-around unique.

GOOD

WESTVIEW PROMENADE
BY
★ ★ J.P. BROOKS ★ ★
Live in a Tropical Paradise surrounded by palm trees and never-ending flower gardens with highly up-graded 3BD, 2½ BA home, 1½ yrs new, 1950 sq. ft. Plan 150 offers a large fam. rm, with room to spare.
Won't last at $329,000! Open house Sat/Sun by owner 123-4567 ext 000 days, 765-4321 eves & wknds.

Fig. 3A

POOR

3 BDRM
2½ BTH home with large fam. rm. Upgrd carpeting upgrade floors, wooden blinds. In WESTVIEW PROMENADE. Mirrored closet doors. 1½ years old with nice landscaping. For sale by owner. 987-6543.

GOOD

★ "LAKES" CONDO ★
NORTHERN ESTATES
2 BR, 2BA+ fam. rm. w/plenty of living space! Unbelievable upgrades with cedar and oak. The most spectacular "Lakes" condo ever offered! By owner $141,900., 765-4321 ex-001 wkdys, 123-456 eves & wknds.

Fig. 3B

POOR

• FOR SALE BY OWNER •
Condo at the 'Lakes'– 2BD, 2BA cedar and oak upgrades in NORTH-ERN estates. Good price $141,9000, ph 012-3456.

GOOD

★ PARK PLACE HILLS ★
• Magnificent Pool Home •
One of the finest pool homes you will find! Crystal blue waters come with this 4BD, 3 BTH home. Highly upgraded w/hdwd flrs & neutral carpets. 4TH bdrm converted to den. BY OWN-ER $244,900. Open house Sat/Sun. 123-4567 ext-000 days, 765-4321 eves & wknds.

Fig. 3C

POOR

FOR SALE – Nice home in Park Place Hills. 3BD + den, 3 bths. Oak floors w/tan carpets. Pool in back yard. Call 123-4567.

Ad #3C has the following unique features:

✓"Park Place Hills" - (location) is a superior place to live.

✓Magnificent Pool Home" - Home has a superior pool and setting.

✓"Highly upgraded" - home is highly decorated.

If your home, in your opinion, is unattractive and needs a lot of work, then you still have a unique feature. You have a fixer-upper and you have a home that is in high demand! There are many people out there who are handy at fixing things and are looking for a home just like yours. They will be expecting to pay a bit less for your home for their efforts. If this sounds like your home, then price it accordingly and build on this feature. You can use such phrases as "Absolutely the best value to be found!" and "Won't last!" Even use phrases like "Unbelievable Savings," "Your palace in disguise," "Handyman's dream," or "If you like fixer-uppers, then here is your chance!"

If your home needs a lot of work, then you still have a unique feature. You have a fixer-upper and you have a home that is in high demand!

Now, before you begin to write your own ad, here are just a few last recommendations before moving on.

- Notice the use of stars and dots in the ads. The use of these symbols becomes a real attention-getter and helps center and visually balance the ad.

- Always list a price in the ad. This has always been an age-old controversy in advertising, but you, as a party selling your own home, should not be too concerned with controversy. You should be concerned that by omitting the price:

✓some readers will not call, for they feel that a house that is as beautiful as it appears in the ad must be more than they can afford.

✓some readers will call who truly cannot afford to buy your house. After the price is revealed, their embarrassment will cause them either to hang up or lead you on.

✓many readers will not call at all.

✓If you are planning an open house the following weekend, place this fact in the ad. This can prove to be very effective. It allows a prospective buyer to connect the mental picture that he has created from your ad to the actual picture of your home - without an appointment or commitment.

✓If the newspaper that you plan to advertise in is a daily paper, check the discount rates for running several consecutive days. If this is more than you care to spend, run Sunday only.

✓Call your local city newspaper. Many of them run weekly only, and the advertising rate may be significantly less.

WRITING YOUR SALES FLIER
Planning and moving ahead for a minute, your ad has been placed. You have received phone calls from prospective buyers, and you have shown your home to these prospective buyers. You will want to give them something to take with them which continues your sales efforts. It will give these potential buyers something to read and comprehend after their visit and will give them information they may have missed during their visit. Most importantly, however, it will give them something that will continue to inspire, motivate, and emotionally overwhelm them. This is your sales flier.

Remove those features which may not truly be positive features, such as "immediate freeway access," "view of playground," or "recently repaired ceilings,"

Your sales flier will consist, primarily, of the information that was used in your newspaper ad but will give you a chance to explain in detail each and every feature your home has to offer. It must be written with the same emotional impact (if not more) that was displayed in your ad.

Focus around the unique features your home has to offer and then list all features your home offers. To help you in writing this flier, start by making a list of every detail that describes your home, beginning with the number of bedrooms and bathrooms and following through to the smallest of upgrades. Once this list is complete, review it, this time wearing an editor's cap, and become selective. Remove those features which may not truly be positive features, such as "immediate freeway access," "view of playground," or "recently repaired ceilings," as these may point out shortcomings elsewhere. Use the same attention-getting words and phrases that were covered in writing your newspaper ad. Create a brief summarizing introduction about your home and continue by listing the features your home offers in order of declining importance or uniqueness. Place the price (same as listed in your ad) and your phone numbers at the bottom. You may want to dig up a floor plan of your home from an old sales brochure or house plan and use a copy of it as a second page for your flier. It creates a finishing touch and allows your prospective buyer to start mentally arranging his furniture in what may be his new home.

Once your sales flier is complete, type it or have it typed, and take it to your local copy shop and have copies made. The use of colored paper will give it that professional look. A sample of a successful sales flier has been shown on the next page.

(Sales Flyer)
(Sample)

** WESTVIEW PROMENADE **
by J.P. Brooks
12345 Pine Lane, Irvine

Offered is plan 260; 3 bedrooms, 2 1/2 baths + family room, 1950 sq.ft.
Home is situated on a private driveway in a very private setting. Probably
the most complete and custom landscaped unit to be found! Home is
absolutely ready to provide a carefree California lifestyle!

INTERIOR

* Rare covered exterior entry
* Hardwood oak entry and family room floors
* Mirrored dining room wall, ceiling to floor, side to side
* Mirrored wardrobe closet doors
* Built-in trash compactor
* Built-in microwave oven
* Custom wooden blinds throughout with matching custom draperies
* Plantation shutters between living room and family room
* Heavy duty shelving in garage
* Upgraded neutral color carpet
* Fire protection system throughout home, including automatic fire
  alarm
* Forced air conditioning and heating
* Garage door opener

EXTERIOR

* Completely landscaped in a lush tropical setting including, palm trees,
  banana trees, and never-ending flower gardens.
* Two raised concrete decks (wired for fountains) with brick trim and
  inlay and matching walkways all lavishly covered with outdoor
  carpeting.
* Automatic sprinklers, front and rear, for worry-free maintenance.
* Automatic lighting systems in front, side, and rear yards.

  Association pools, spas, and recreational parks available to all
  Westview residents.

This breathtaking home is being offered at $329,900.

Evenings and weekends PH (123) 765-4321
Weekdays   PH (765) 123-4567 Ext. 000

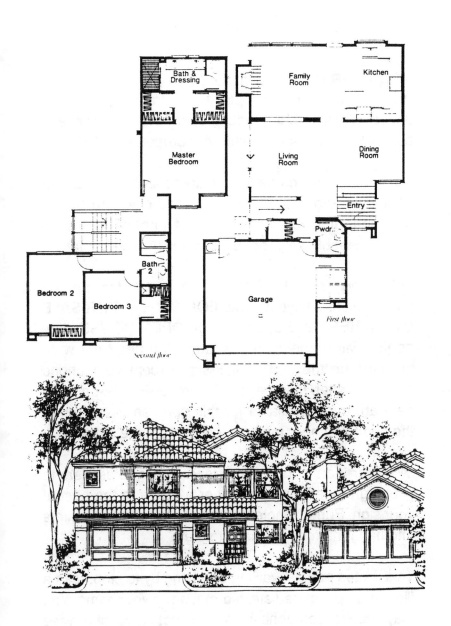

Bath &
Dressing

Family
Room

Kitchen

Master
Bedroom

Living
Room

Dining
Room

Entry

Pwdr.

Bedroom 2

Bath
2

Bedroom 3

Garage

First floor

Second floor

YOUR FOR SALE SIGN

You now need a sign to place in a strategic location in the front (and/or rear) of your property to inform passers-by to know intentions to sell your property.

Some communities have restrictions as to the number of signs, the placement of signs, and even the size of the sign. It is best to check, if uncertain, with a knowledgeable neighbor or community representative.

Visit your local hardware store and select an appropriate sign, saying either FOR SALE or FOR SALE BY OWNER. Also select a large OPEN HOUSE sign, as you will be needing this later. You need not write anything on the FOR SALE sign except your phone number written in large, black numbers. Stick-on numbers are even available for this purpose. Remember, the phone number must be legible from the street.

A clever idea is to attach a few of your sales fliers to your sign by attaching a nail or a screw to the post of your sign. Punch a hole through the top of several fliers and hang them on the nail or screw.

This invites people walking or driving by to stop, take a flier, and gain immediate information on your home. You may inspire someone who may not have otherwise stopped by. A great number of homes have been sold over the years solely as a result of the FOR SALE sign seen by those passing by.

...attach a few of your sales fliers to your sign by attaching a nail or a screw to the post of your sign.

CHAPTER IV

THE SPLIT

The subject of this chapter may catch you by surprise and most likely will not reflect your true intentions. Never the less, you must be educated in this matter in order to adequately anticipate and prepare for your response. This is the matter of the realtor/owner split.

As you advertise By Owner in the newspapers and display By Owner signs in your yard, you will be stirring a great amount of attention from realtors. You will now be a duly authorized, officially sworn, real honest-to-goodness FSBO (For Sale By Owner), pronounced in the industry: fiz'bo. The term FSBO to the professional real estate industry, tends toward a mildly negative connotation, just as a non- professional in any industry may tend to threaten the professional when he claims he can perform the same function.

It is also known by realtors, however, that the FSBO represents opportunity. Similarly, the realtor may represent opportunity for the FSBO. The realtor may become your best friend during the course of selling your home. You may even find that during the course of your For-Sale-By-Owner campaign the association with realtors in some phase or another becomes a major part of your efforts.

Real estate firms earn their profits from two basic categories: selling properties and listing properties. Some realtors earn their wages strictly from selling properties, and some strictly from listing properties. A good number of realtors earn their wages from both.

"No, I am not interested in listing my home at this time, but if you truly have a buyer for my home, I will consider offering a finder's fee."

Think for a minute of the realtor attempting to acquire a listing. How does he find people who are ready to sell their home but haven't yet listed with an agency? Well, there are many techniques that we need not go into, except for one. What better method to find potential listings than to read through the newspapers and locate FSBO's? They have the desire to sell their home but have not listed with an agency. Many of the calls that you receive just may be from such realtors.

The realtor will undoubtedly ask you if you are cooperating with brokers.

The conversation may sound something like this:

"Hello, I'm calling about the home that you have for sale." (Now he has your attention.) "I'm John Smith from the XYZ Real Estate firm. I was calling to see if we could offer you assistance in marketing your home. We currently have a buyer for a home like yours and I feel that we could do a great job marketing it..." and so on. Your answer should be: "No, I'm not interested in listing my home at this time." A second back-up answer may be (after carefully considering the possibilities found in this chapter) "No, I am not interested in listing my home at this time, but if you truly have a buyer for my home, I will consider offering a finder's fee." The conversation will most likely end here, or he may attempt to make an appointment to preview your home. In either case, you will probably be hearing from him again; plan on it within a month.

...the realtor knows that if he tries to sway his customer away from the open house, his customer may return on his own, and the realtor may lose him.

If during an open house, you find that you have a realtor, accompanied by his customer, previewing your home, you may have whole different ball game. As mentioned previously, a realtor showing property will usually display reluctance when it comes to his customer and a FSBO Open House. He knows that if he tries to sway his customer away from the open house, his customer may return on his own, and the realtor may lose him. The realtor will, therefore, reluctantly assist his customer in previewing the open house and hope for the best. The realtor will undoubtedly ask you if you are cooperating with brokers. What this means is, are you willing to split the usual six percent real estate commission with the broker if his customer wants to buy your house? In different terms, are you willing to pay three percent commission or some negotiated amount as commission (it could be smaller) to sell your house to their customer? Keep in mind that if a real estate firm sells a listed home, and the home is not their listing, they will receive a three percent commission (based on the average of six percent total) for their sales efforts. If their office deals with you as a FSBO and they offer a split, then they would be making no less than if they had sold another agency's listed home.

You must carefully consider this option ahead of time so you can be prepared with a firm answer if the situation arises.

If your answer is a definite no, and if the realtor truly has a strong and interested buyer, then you may be involuntarily forcing a situation in which the customer makes an attempt to betray his realtor and comes directly to you. This can result in a very messy and entangled situation, and I suggest it be avoided.

Your best answer may probably be: "Maybe we can work something out,"

Your best answer may probably be: "Maybe we can work something out," which suggests the future possibility of a negotiated agreement that both you and the real estate agency could be happy with.

In the event that you were to decide to create some form of a split agreement with the agency, you will probably be asked to sign a single party listing. This will basically state that your home will be listed with the agency only if the stated customer wishes to buy your home. It will also state the negotiated real estate commission that you and the agency have agreed to, and will establish a time period in which it will remain effective.

The split will be an option that you must consider very carefully. It will require a decision that will not be easy to make. You may find it easier to reach such a decision only after the specific instance has come up, and you have already become acquainted with both the realtor and his client.

Being an F.S.B.O. puts you in the best negotiating position.

IF YOU DECIDE TO SPLIT
✓You will have saved and made yourself half or more of the real estate commission that you would have otherwise saved completely.

✓Your sales campaign will be over at this point, for the real estate agency will take care of all necessary paperwork.

✓Consider the split to be a compromise between a full listing and a complete For Sale By Owner campaign.

IF YOU DECIDE NOT TO SPLIT
✓You will have saved yourself a complete real estate commission per your original plans.

✓You will allow yourself the opportunity to carry out the remainder of your For Sale By Owner campaign as planned.

✓You will benefit from the experience and confidence gained for future For Sale By Owner ventures.

CHAPTER V

THE OPEN HOUSE

Another method of recruiting or connecting with potential buyers is through what is commonly called the open house, that is, opening up your home and allowing others, without the need for an appointment, to preview the home.

Much can be said about open houses in that they can inspire and excite a prospective buyer, by seeing the home as it is lived in and feeling its warmth. He can feel the sense of security that a home provides and smell the grass and the flowers around it. As stressed many times before, it is a time to emotionally overwhelm the prospective buyer. A successful open house; however, does not merely exist by opening up the door. This emotion that you are looking to sell must be created.

You will find the largest concentration of people coming between 11:00 AM and 3:00 PM...

By now, your home should be at a point where it is ready to sell, and all of those details that were discussed earlier about creating curb appeal and first impressions should have been put into place. It is now time to turn up the heat!

The Best Time

You will undoubtedly want to select the best time to hold your open house to bring in the greatest number of people. Once again, a home can be seen and sold on any day of the week, but plan your first few open houses on Saturday and Sunday. You will find the largest concentration of people coming between 11:00 AM and 3:00 PM; however, it only takes one buyer and he may be the one who has been looking at houses all day, and happened to stumble upon yours at 4:45 PM.

The professional real estate industry conducts preview open houses during the week, and that particular day of the week is usually consistent within a given area. They call this day Caravan Day and its intent is to allow all persons associated with the real estate industry to view the interior of newly listed homes. You may want to take advantage of some of the traffic of Caravan Day by opening up your house during this event.

There may be an intense fumbling for your listing between agencies and in doing so expose the existence of a new, beautiful home for sale.

This type of open house is usually a bit special in that some form of food and beverages are served. Keep an eye out in your neighborhood for a day in which many homes are displaying flags and open house signs. This will be caravan day and can be your day also.

Expect mostly realtors to be walking through, and expect their attempts at gaining your listing. Use the techniques that were previously discussed to resist. Your intentions for opening up your home on this day are to:

1) Gain Exposure - even though realtors know that you are selling by owner, and especially if your house has a great amount of curb appeal, the realtor may become your greatest ally by indirectly spreading the word about the availability of your home. There may be an intense fumbling for your listing between agencies and in doing so expose the existence of a new, beautiful home for sale.

2) Make Contacts - by opening up your home you will be meeting people and thereby making friends. With these friends you will now have contacts; many of them may open up to you and offer you their support, if needed. You may find this comforting. You may even find that your new friends wind up rooting for you.

3) Build a safety net - By creating new friends and contacts you open yourself up to a greater possibility (but only if absolutely desired by you) of a more desirable split or finder's fee negotiation in the future.

Walk through your home and turn on every single light.

Begin Your Open House

It is now time to open up your home. If you had mentioned in your newspaper ad that your house would be open on that day, expect to meet the parties with whom you have already had conversations.

Now, think of a model home that you may have recently visited and think of how it overwhelmed you. What did you see?

Walk through your home and turn on every single light. This includes closet lights, bathroom lights, desk lamps, dining room chandelier, ceiling lights...everything! Now, open every interior door. If you have walk-in closets with doors and they are in an orderly state, then open those. If it is a cold day, light the fireplace and turn on the heat to a nice toasty comfort level. If it is a hot day, turn on the air conditioning.

If you have no air conditioning, open every screened window. Turn on your stereo. Find a station that plays soft, mellow music and set the volume to a low, barely audible level. Even if you do not like this music, bear with it. It will create a more effective home-selling atmosphere.

Open every drape or window covering. If you have blinds, leave them down but open up the slats to allow for the most light.

The open house can appeal to the sense of smell as well.

Straighten up crooked pictures on the wall, close all toilet lids, pick up loose newspapers, mail, or magazines, and remove small valuable items that are eye catching or setting out in the open. Vacuum central areas to create a fresh look, and place your sales flier on a table in the entry. Now, stop and catch your breath....

If you have purchased flags, place them on your property near the street. Balloons work well for this purpose and are a real attention-getter.

Place your open house sign in a strategic location on your property, near the street. If you have purchased open house directional signs (with arrows), place them at locations in your neighborhood that direct traffic to your home. If you have purchased flags, place them on your property near the street. Balloons work well for this purpose and are a real attention-getter. Tie them to your open house sign. Return inside your home and leave the front door ajar, but not open. Now pick up a good book or find something, not too involved, to keep yourself busy. If you or your spouse are handy in the kitchen, bake something simple that will create a nice homey smell (like cookies, bread, etc.) The open house can appeal to the sense of smell as well.

As people knock on the door and enter your home, greet them with a smile. They need to feel as though they are welcome and not intruding. This could be their new home! Offer them a sales flier. Be friendly and talk to them, but do not follow them around. You will know how comfortable you feel with each party and how closely you feel you need to keep an eye out. It's best to give them the freedom they need and the privacy to talk, but know where they are at all times.

After they have had some time to become familiar with your home, but prior to movements that suggest that they are about to leave, ask them something like this: "Well, what do you think?" or "Can I answer any questions?" You will want to take this time (as this is your sales time) to explain some of the features on your sales flier, or show them unique and exciting features about your home that they may have missed. If you find that they have a particular area of focus, place your area of focus there also. If you have a pool and they appear to be intrigued by it, tell them something exciting about it.

"Yes, when we built this pool, we designed it around a waterfall we saw when we...." If they are intrigued by a particular view, then you could say something like: "Yes, we just love it here. On a crisp day, we sit here drinking our coffee and look out over those mountains." In short, place your attention where their attention is. If you display your enthusiasm about your home, you will inspire their enthusiasm and, therefore, generate interest on their part.

You may find that, after talking to your guests, they were looking for a four bedroom home, and you have three bedrooms. They may tell you they must have a family room, and you do not. They might also say the price is way out of their range or state some other insurmountable problem which cannot be overcome. Do not become frustrated. There may be many of these. This is their way of either speaking the truth or politely letting you know that they are not interested.

It is not uncommon that people will leave and, for a period of time, read your flier over and over again.

Continue to be friendly and courteous and be sure they still have your sales flier to take with them. Say something like, "Thanks so much for stopping by, and if I can be of any help, I'll be here. My number is on the flier if you need to reach me." It is not uncommon that people will leave and, for a period of time, read your flier over and over again. They may have been overwhelmed by one particular feature of your home and then later become obsessed by it. They will then find a way to mentally or physically overcome that insurmountable obstacle (add a room, remove that tree, borrow extra money from the in-laws, etc.). We've seen even the largest of insurmountable obstacles overcome strictly as a result of the emotional appeal a certain feature had on the buyer. They could be back at your door at any time! This is why it is so very important to maintain that friendly and courteous rapport with your customer even after you have been disappointed with their seemingly hopeless requirements.

Always keep a copy of your sales flier by the telephone and use it at this time as a guide.

Showing Your Home By Appointment

When a prospective buyer calls from your newspaper ad, or maybe he pulled your number from the For Sale sign out in front, they will probably ask you to tell them a little something about your home. This is your chance to give your sales talk.

Always keep a copy of your sales flier by the telephone and use it at this time as a guide. Talk about the outstanding and unique features that your home has to offer. Use a positive tone of voice (to prove that you truly believe it yourself) and speak with the same eye-catching words that you used in your ad. In this case it will become ear catching. "Yes, Mr. Jones, I believe that my home has absolutely the finest landscaping you will find in this neighborhood!" In reality your landscaping may not be absolutely the best, but it certainly may be nice enough to boast about.

Talking about your home's unique and outstanding features is stressed because this gains the attention and arouses the emotions of your listener. You may have only a limited amount of talking time, so proceed by painting an overall picture of your home. You may want to talk about size, exact location, or facts that otherwise may not have been covered in the ad.

Some prospective buyers are timid, noncommittal, and would rather just see you at the open house.

It's now your caller's turn to talk. They will either respond by showing interest, or as discussed earlier, will respond with some fact that becomes an obstacle in pursuing it further. If it is the latter, then with a friendly voice simply say, "Well, Mr. Jones, if I can be of any help to you, just call, and I will be more than happy to show you the property at your convenience." If your caller shows interest and asks if you are planning an open house in the near future, say yes and when. Some prospective buyers are timid, noncommittal, and would rather just see you at the open house.

Make a good attempt, however, to schedule a personal appointment.

This way you can assure a one-on-one arrangement without distractions.

If your caller asks to see your home, by all means, don't wait for an open house!

Make an appointment with them then—even that night, if possible. It may be inconvenient for you, but it could mean a possible sale.

When showing your home by appointment, you will use identical techniques as those used during your open house. In other words, turn all lights on, light the fireplace, vacuum main areas of carpet, etc., all those little details as discussed earlier that "ice the cake". You will have an advantage this time, however. Your prospective buyer already knows a little about your home and arrives in a somewhat anxious state of mind. Use this to your advantage. Paste that smile on your face, greet them with a friendly welcome, hand them a sales flier, and proceed as if you were holding an open house.

CHAPTER VI

THE OFFER

Your prospective buyer may be an experienced homebuyer, or at least present themself to be. On the other hand, they may be inexperienced and know very little. It is my intention that you learn and become familiar with enough information about both buying and selling homes that you can deal intelligently with any situation that may come up.

The escrow company handles legal matters for which realtors often get credit—so don't be intimidated!

When a prospective buyer desires to purchase a home, they will most always desire to purchase the home at a price less than the asking price. When a home is listed with a real estate agency, and this buyer wishes to offer a lower amount for the home, a document is drawn up. This document is used as an offer but is drawn up as a real estate purchase contract and receipt for deposit. This document is generally involved. It contains information about the buyer and information about desired financing. It includes the price the buyer is offering to purchase the home, and most importantly, is accompanied by a check from the buyer to act as a deposit. The amount of this deposit can be anywhere in the neighborhood of one percent to three percent of the purchase price of the home. If the seller agrees with the price and terms of the offer, then the offer is accepted and the house is sold. If the seller does not accept the terms of the offer, then he can respond through his agency with a counteroffer. This is another document that basically states those conditions the seller will accept. It goes on from there until seller and buyer reach agreeable terms. A key point here is that the offer is accompanied by a deposit of a sizable amount.

You, as a For Sale By Owner, will not be dealing with written offers, unless you end up in some fashion dealing with an agent. The offers that you deal with will be far less complicated and will be verbal.

You will not be receiving a deposit until an offer is accepted.

Your prospective buyer, if they are experienced in working with For Sale By Owners, may realize the informal nature of such offers and may attempt to take advantage of the situation and may say something like, "What's the lowest price you will accept?"

Or, "Will you take $XXX,XXX?" You must not give in to this line of questioning! You should respond with: "If you are truly interested in buying my home, then we can sit down and talk." If they are experienced, they may be trying to bait you or feel you out to determine how flexible you are with your pricing. If they are not experienced, then they are probably just asking. In either case, your answer shall remain the same. There is great significance to the phrase "sit down and talk."

"Sit down" carries with it a form of commitment, a sense of seriousness. Did you ever sign a contract or close a big deal standing up? You need room to spread out, shuffle papers around, and a surface to write on. If your prospective buyer is willing to sit down and talk with you, then you know you have a truly interested buyer.

They may ask you the exact size of a room (they are mentally moving in furniture).

You are holding an open house, or you are showing a party your home by appointment. You have given this party your sales flier, and they have had a chance to look at your home. You have taken the opportunity to speak with them and present them your pep talk. How do you know they are interested? They may ask you questions about a feature of your house. They may ask you questions about your flier. They may ask you the exact size of a room (they are mentally moving in furniture). The party may sit down in a particular room to get a better feel for your home. They may walk out to the back or front yard and look back at the house. They will open the kitchen cabinet doors to determine the space they will have. They will show signs of moving themselves in.

If your party says, "We like it!" or "Where do we go from here?" these are the words that you are waiting to hear. If they say "We are very interested but...." and some obstacle is mentioned, make an attempt to help them overcome the obstacle. Say things like "That tree can be removed" or "The back yard is large enough for a nice size pool!" This can truly sway the borderline buyer!

If their only obstacle appears to be the price of your home, and you feel they are truly interested, then it's time to sit down and talk!

We have included a sales agreement in the Appendices for you to enlarge and photocopy or print from.

This is the beginning of the period of your home selling venture in which an inexperienced buyer will feel lost. They will not know which way to turn, what to sign and not to sign, and so on. This is the period in which even the most experienced buyer may become so emotionally overwhelmed with their purchase or near purchase that they go into a state of shock which prevents them from thinking clearly. This is the period when you must take charge! Preparedness is the best way for you to master this feat, be knowledgeable of a few simple principles.

Prior to this nitty-gritty phase you should make a trip to the local stationery store. Purchase a Mortgage Payment Tables guide (or equivalent), which is a small book listing loan payment schedules at various interest rates for various payback periods. You should also buy at least three real estate sales agreement forms. This form will also be called Real Estate Purchase Contract and Receipt For Deposit. If your local stationery store does not carry a form like this, (most of them do, however) then ask them to order you some. A sample of one of these forms has been included in the appendices of this book.

This exercise of sitting down will also allow your prospective buyers to feel as though they are actually purchasing your home and will most likely motivate and excite them.

You should also make a trip to your local savings and loan institution or a bank that you feel comfortable with. Ask someone in the loan department for several real estate loan applications and inquire about the different loan programs. They will probably give you a brochure explaining these programs. It is not our intent for you to become anything close to a loan expert, but merely that you have knowledge of basic loan parameters and their criteria. This will allow you the advantage and enable you to guide your buyers when needed.

Your buyers are truly interested in your home, and their only hesitation appears to focus around the purchase price of your home. They have not yet made an offer on you home. It is extremely helpful, at this point to sit down with these potential buyers and go through the numbers with them. This will enable them to get a true feel for what exactly your home will cost them. Base your numbers breakdown on your asking price. Your buyers, in the back of their minds, will know that whatever numbers you come up with they can assume to be lower. They know they would probably be purchasing your home at a number less than your asking price. This exercise of sitting down will also allow your prospective buyers to feel as though they are actually purchasing your home and will most likely motivate and excite them. Offer them a cup of coffee or tea to help them feel comfortable.

Let's say the asking price of your home is $187,900. Obtain a large pad of paper to use for your calculations. Present to your buyers a program something like the following: (Your verbiage will be noted in quotations)

"Let's take a look at what you will be spending for this home." "We'll use $187,900 as a starting figure and work from there." "Can you tell me what number you feel comfortable with as a down payment?"

They may respond with a number, or may respond with a percentage. "Can you also tell me whether you feel comfortable with an adjustable rate mortgage (ARM) or a fixed rate mortgage?" If they do not understand the difference, then explain to them the following in the simplest of terms:

Adjustable Rate Mortgage - A loan program in which the interest rate will vary or float in parallel with an interest rate of a given, specified, and published index. There are usually ceilings associated with the interest rate to prevent the rate from climbing or lowering indefinitely. Since the interest rate is allowed to adjust, the bank will be assured of carrying a loan that will always reflect a current rate of interest.

See the Glossary for more terms.

The starting rate of this program is therefore considerably lower than that of a fixed rate mortgage and thus easier for a party to qualify.

Fixed Rate Mortgage - A loan program in which the interest rate will remain fixed or at the same value throughout the life of the loan.

You should also understand the following terms:

Loan-to-Value Ratio - Banks will lend only a percentage of the purchase price (market value) of the property. The balance of the complete amount will be contributed by the buyer and is known as the down payment or owner's equity. The banks may vary the interest rates and terms of the loan based on the percentage that the buyer contributes.

See the Glossary for more terms.

Generally, the higher the percentage that the buyer places down, the more favorable will be the loan terms, and the easier the qualifying process. The loan-to-value-ratio refers to the bank's contribution (loan amount) divided by the purchase price (or market value) of the home. This will equal a percentage (90 percent, 80 percent, 70 percent, etc.).

In general terms, 90 percent will be the maximum amount the banks will loan to a qualified buyer. Loans can be made of even higher values, but they are extremely rare and require nearly perfect credit.

Closing Costs - Your estimate will result in greater accuracy if you include buyer's closing costs. They consist primarily of loan fees, recording fees, escrow fees, etc., and can be estimated as a percentage of the loan amount. This percentage usually runs into the range of 2 1/2 percent - 3 percent (use 3 percent to be conservative).

»   Note: Closing cost estimates, when used on your worksheet, will determine a closer value of your buyer's true costs.

Often closing costs are ignored in the early purchase phase of home selling, and when these figures are finally added in, the buyer may become frustrated, shocked, or otherwise short of funds. The closing costs that you estimate on your worksheet will not, however, be included in your agreement to sell real estate contract between the buyer and yourself. These actual costs will be determined and specified by the bank and escrow company.

Since this 3 three percent closing cost estimate is a percentage of the loan amount, and the loan amount at this point is unknown, use the following guideline and formula to calculate a down payment amount which includes closing costs:

Purchase Price -   known (or assumed)

(+) Closing Costs -   unknown (3 percent of what?)

(-) Down Payment -   known

= Loan Amount -   unknown

Because of unknowns involved, this problem would be difficult to solve. Through the miracle of mathematics, however, this problem can be rearranged into a simple formula:

Purchase Price

(-)   Down Payment

<u>(Divide)   .97</u>

=   Loan Amount

(In words:) Subtract the down payment from the purchase price = loan amount price. Divide by .97. This will give you the loan amount.

In the event that your prospective buyer has given you a percentage as a down payment rather than a dollar amount, simply multiply that percentage by the purchase price. Example: 20 percent down would be .20 x $187,900 = $37,580.

Your worksheet will look like:

WORKSHEET FOR BUYER
- Down Payment -

$187,900.00	Purchase Price
-$30,000.00	Down Payment
$157,900.00	Sub-Total
<u>.97</u>	<u>Closing Costs</u>

(3 percent of loan amount, approximately)

$162,783.50   Total loan amount,
($157,900.00 ÷ .97)   (approximately)

» Note: To determine directly the value for the closing costs (you will need this later during your sale), multiply the total loan amount by 3 percent (.03). This amount will eventually be subtracted from the total down payment as you write up your sales contract.

Example:

$162,783.00	Total Loan Amount
x.03 = $4,883.49	Estimated Closing Costs

Now to determine the loan to value ratio to assure that the loan amount does not exceed 90 percent),

divide $162,783	Loan Amount
by $187,900	purchase price
= .866 or 86.6 percent	
Loan-to-value-ratio =	86.6 percent

If the loan to value ratio were to exceed 90 percent, then one of two factors must change: a larger down payment is needed or a reduction in the purchase price amount.

If everything is in order thus far and your buyers appear to have, or have access to, a sufficient down payment, then proceed with the next worksheet on loan details. For the purpose of this discussion, and based on recent averages, 8 percent will be used as the interest rate for the adjustable rate mortgage and 10 percent will be used for the fixed rate mortgage. The life, or term, of the average loan is usually 30 years and will be used in the example.

WORKSHEET FOR BUYER
- Loan Details -

Adjustable Rate Mortgage	Fixed Rate Mortgage
$162,783 - Total Loan Amount	$162,783 - Total Loan Amount
30 Years - Term of Loan	30 Years - Term of Loan
8 percent - Starting Interest Rate	10 percent - Interest Rate
Payment = $1,193/month Payment	= $1,427/month
(Calculated)	(Calculated)

The monthly payment of the given loan amount is determined by use of the mortgage payment tables guide. This guide is usually arranged by pages of increasing interest rates. The term is displayed horizontally from one to forty years and the loan amount is displayed vertically. When dealing with uneven loan amounts, simple addition will be required. The monthly payment for the above loan amount of $162,783 is determined as follows:

Locate the page which lists the given interest amount (of 8 percent) at the top. Read sideways and locate the given term (30 years). Read down and locate the loan amount or nearest loan amount. In this example, and depending on your particular guide, the exact monthly payment will be determined by adding five separate loan amounts: $100,000, $60,000, $2,000, $700, and $75, and adding together the individual monthly payments.

$100,000	$733.77/month
$60,000	$440.26/month
$2,000	$ 14.68/month
$700	$ 5.14/month
$75	$ .56/month

($75 is the closest number to $83)

$162,775 = $1,194.41

The total monthly payment for the loan amount of $162,783 at 8 percent interest is $1,194.

Similarly, the calculations for the same loan amount for the 10 percent fixed rate mortgage are as follows:

$100,000	$ 877.58/month
$60,000	$ 526.55/month
$2,000	$ 17.56/month
$700	$ 6.15/month
$75	$ .66/month

$162,775 = $1,428.50/month

The total monthly payment for the loan amount of $162,783 at 10 percent interest is $1,428.

» Special Note: Business/financial calculators are available to perform such calculations and require an investment of around $30 - $40. This could be a sound investment and could help in the future.

You will find that the entire process of creating worksheets for your prospective buyers will motivate both you and your buyers by the mere opportunity to work with the numbers and talk about your home. You will also discover that both you and your buyers will gain a great deal of insight into their ability to purchase your home. It is for these reasons that the worksheet at this stage becomes such an effective sales tool in the actual selling of your home.

You are not the bank, but you have a right to know if you are dealing with a qualified party.

There is one last matter to discuss regarding the prequalifying of your prospective buyers and this is the matter of income and debt ratio. Though this matter can be discussed after the offer and sale, it will be to your advantage to discuss it now with your buyers, as you will gain further valuable insight into their buying capabilities.

You may feel somewhat uncomfortable in bringing up such matters as income with your prospective buyers. This is normal. If you feel they are not ready, then do not force the issue. You will find, however, that given they are truly interested in your property, most buyers will not hesitate in the least in providing information to you about their income. By this time, you have won their confidence and they will be looking to you as someone who is sincerely trying to help them. You need to acquire a feel for your buyer's income, as you need to acquire a feel for what is known as their debt ratio.

The bank will be doing this, and it gives you a chance to prequalify your buyers. You are not the bank, but you have a right to know if you are dealing with a qualified party. It will help you determine how flexible you can be with your sale in general.

In general terms, the debt ratio refers to the proportion of gross monthly income which is used for major debts. This ratio is expressed as a percentage and is determined by dividing the major debt monthly expense by the gross monthly income.

Lenders will look at two types of debt ratios and issue loans such that both these ratios are satisfied. These two ratios are as follows:

Front-End Ratio - The proportion of monthly real estate expenses (loan payments, taxes, and insurance) to gross monthly income.

Back-End Ratio - The proportion of monthly real estate expenses plus long tern debt to gross monthly income.

Long term debt usually consists of all debts which require scheduled payments of a period lasting longer than ten months. Examples would be personal loans, car loans, credit card balances, etc.

Lending institutions take both of these types of debt ratios into consideration when evaluating a loan request and combine them with all of the other variables to reach their decision. These other variables include overall credit status, the size of the down payment (creating the loan-to-value ratio), type of loan, length of employment, etc. Every loan request that they receive is, therefore, totally unique and is considered on an individual basis.

Your intentions shall only be to establish general qualifications based on general average figures. Average ranges in which the banks seek are as follows:

Adjustable Rate Loan - Less than 20 percent Down (higher than 80 percent Loan To Value Ratio)

Front-End Ratio - Up to 33 percent - 36 percent

Back-End Ratio - Up to 38 percent - 41 percent

Adjustable-Rate Loan - 20 percent down or more (80 percent or lower Loan To Value Ratio

Front-End Ratio - Up to 33 percent - 38 percent

Back-End Ratio - Up to 38 percent - 48 percent

Fixed Rate Loan - All Loan Amounts

> Front-End Ratio - Up to 33 percent - 35 percent

> Back-End Ratio - Up to 38 percent - 39 percent

We suggest that you start with and limit your pre-qualification to the use of the front-end ratio. The information that you will need to know is basically the monthly payment and your buyer's gross monthly income. If your buyers are a married couple and they both work, then be sure to include both incomes in the gross monthly income. You need not explore any further into your buyer's financial history. If they possess and are concerned with their large debt obligations, they will most often volunteer this information. If this is the case, then apply the back-end ratio. Using the example, here is how you will perform the calculation:

Assume the buyer is comfortable with the adjustable rate loan and $30,000 as a down payment. Assume he has given to you a gross monthly income figure of $4,000.

> $1,194/month   monthly payment

> (from your work sheet)

(+) $125/month   real estate taxes

> (use your monthly tax obligation for this purpose or apply the percentage factor typical of your area)

(+)	$25/month	insurance (use your monthly
	_____	insurance obligation here)
=	$1,344/month	Total Housing Costs/Month
Divide	$1,344	Total Housing Costs/month
by	$4,000	Gross Monthly Income
=	.336, or 33.6, (%)	Debt Ratio

Apply this percentage of 33.6 percent to the range for adjustable rate loans of higher than 80 percent (the loan to value ratio from your work sheet was 86.6 percent). The range is 33 percent to 36 percent. This means that the lending institution will consider as a maximum debt ratio anywhere between 33 percent and 36 percent, depending on the buyer's qualifications. In this case the ratio is 33.6 percent and the buyer should be reasonable safe.

Loan Assumptions

In today's economy, interest rates seem to change as quickly as the day turns to night. In a short time frame the changes may be insignificant. Over a longer time period, however, the changes may be substantial.

You may have chosen a time period to sell your home in which the interest rates are very high.

You may also have purchased your home, or refinanced your home, in a time period in which the interest rates were very low. If this is the case, and your loan balance is proportionally high, then you may have a valuable sales tool that can help in selling your home. The possibility exists where the buyer of your home can assume your current loan (and loan balance) and pay the difference between the loan balance and your selling price as a down payment. This difference may be higher than some buyers can afford to spend, but can be overcome by additional financing. The monthly payment figures could still add up to be considerably less than a new loan.

If you currently have a high-balance, low-interest loan on your home, and are selling within a market plagued by high interest rates, then give your bank a call. They may be of great help to you in defining the parameters of a loan assumption.

The Offer
You now should have a very good feel for where your potential buyers stand. You have a good insight into their financial background and their ability to purchase your home. They in turn have a good feel for their own ability to purchase your home. If the price of your home had been completely out of the question, they most likely would not have accepted your invitation to sit down and talk. The price was therefore somewhere "in the vicinity." It is now a matter for the potential buyers to

determine whether the price irs right for them, and whether the home is right for them. At this point they will most likely want to "talk it over," or if the buyer is alone, will want to "think it over." In either case, if the buyers decide to talk it over without leaving your home, then they probably have an offer on its way. Give them privacy! If they decide to leave, then allow them the courtesy. If their temptation is real, then they will be back. Ask them if they wouldn't mind leaning their name and phone number. You can call them, if you don't hear from them, and ask them if they have reached a decision.

Your party now has had the chance to think over the matter. Their response will most likely be: "We would like to make you an offer." Your response shall be: "Okay, let's talk!"

From this point on, you the seller, and only you can determine whether the amount and conditions of the offer are right for you.

You can respond with a counteroffer, that is, a compromise between their offer and your price, or simply say yes.

CHAPTER VII

THE SALE

You and your buyer have reached an agreement involving the purchase price and the conditions of the sale of your home. It is now a matter of utmost importance to transform this agreement into a written contract. This contract form you have already acquired from the stationery store and is called a Real Estate Sales Agreement. This contract is also referred to as the Real Estate Purchase Contract and receipt for Deposit. This type of contract is available in a variety of other names and formats, but they all pertain to the sale of real estate and include common terminology.

We have included a sales agreement in the Appendices for you to enlarge and photocopy or print from.

A sample of this type of contract has been included in the appendices of this book. Let's discuss the terminology and clauses that will be used in this contract in the order that they would most likely appear.

Identification of seller and buyer - Simply fill in the party who is selling (your name) and the party who is buying.

Real Estate Sales Agreement
(Sample)

I (We) _____ hereinafter referred to as "Seller"
of _____ County and State hereby enter into an agreement with:
_____ hereinafter referred to as "Buyer"
of _____ County and State on this ___ day of _____ 19___ .

1. I agree to sell my property located at:

   _____
   Street Address

   _____
   City

   _____
   State, Zip Code

   to the Buyer based on conditions set forth in this contract.

2. The legal description of my property is as follows:

   _____
   _____
   _____

3. Buyer agrees to pay the Purchase Price of $_____ and the method of payment shall be:

   a)   Deposit to be held in Trust by _____ in the amount of: $_____

   b)   Approximate Principal Balance on New Loan Amount: $_____
        Mortgage Holder: _____
        Interest Rate: _____
        Term of Loan: _____

   c)   Remainder of Down Payment to be in the amount of: $_____
        or that amount which is required to complete the
        purchase price at Closing.

                                                          Total $_____

4. This contract shall provide for a Closing on or before _____, 19___ .

5. Buyer and Seller agree that all attached fixtures and fittings including window shades, curtains and blinds, wall to wall carpeting, built-in or attached appliances, lighting fixtures, plumbing fixtures and hardware, TV antennas, built-in air cooler and air conditioners, garage door openers, and landscaping are INCLUDED in the sale of this property. No personal property shall be included unless specifically listed here.

   INCLUDED WITH PURCHASE:

   _____
   _____
   _____

6. No other special agreements between Buyer and Seller shall be binding unless stated here.

   SPECIAL CLAUSES OR AGREEMENTS:

   _____
   _____
   _____

Real Estate Sales Agreement

Pursuant to this agreement, standard real estate laws will apply and include, but not be limited to the following:

7. Prorations: Buyer and Seller understand that all charges and revenues that accrue against the property and not yet paid or collected shall be prorated at the time of Closing between the accounts of the Buyer and Seller.

8. Clear Title: Buyer and Seller understand that Seller shall convey to Buyer a clear or marketable title to said property. If such marketable title cannot be obtained, as would be acceptable to a title insurance company or lender, then Seller shall refund to Buyer the Deposit or any consideration placed in connection with this agreement, and contract will be cancelled.

9. Default of Buyer: Buyer and Seller understand that if Buyer fails to perform any conditions of this contract, then Seller may retain the Deposit, or any consideration placed in connection with this contract, as liquidated damages. This agreement will then be cancelled.

10. Default of Seller: Buyer and Seller understand that if Seller fails to perform any conditions of this contract, then Buyer may elect to demand a full refund of the Deposit or any consideration used in connection with this contract, or demand his right to specific performance.

11. Restrictions, Easements, and Limitations: Buyer and Seller understand that Buyer shall take title to said property subject to all Restrictions, Easements, and Limitations that are currently in force.

12. Maintenance: Buyer and Seller understand that Seller shall maintain said property as it currently exists between this date and the date of Closing. Seller is not responsible for the normal result of aging during this time period.

13. Termite Inspection: Buyer and Seller understand that Seller agrees to have premises inspected by a State Licensed Pest Exterminator for live, wood destroying insects, fungus, or wood rot. If such infestation is found, then Seller shall have treated and any visual structural damage repaired. Seller shall be limited to 3% of the purchase price for repairs. If such costs exceed 3%, then the Buyer can elect to pay the difference or forfeit this contract.

14. Walk-Through Inspection: Buyer and Seller agree that Buyer, or his agent, has the right to inspect premises at least 15 days before Closing to determine the working condition of appliances, plumbing, air conditioning and heating system, electrical systems, sprinklers, pool equipment, and roofing. Seller shall pay for repairs as necessary to bring such items into working condition. Buyer has the right to reinspect premises within 48 hours of Closing to assure that repairs have been made. If roofing repairs are required to achieve a watertight condition, then Seller shall be limited to 3% of the purchase price for such repairs. If costs exceed 3%, the Buyer can elect to pay the difference or forfeit this contract.

15. Homeowner's Association: If the property in this transaction belongs to or provides membership in a Homeowner's Association, then copies of its Bylaws and CC&Rs are to be delivered to the Buyer or the above-stated Escrow Company before Closing. The monthly association dues are: $ _____.

16. Unless otherwise stated in the Escrow Instructions, title shall vest as follows: _____

Seller(s):	_____	Buyer(s):	_____
Dated:	_____	Dated:	_____
Address:	_____	Address:	_____
Phone:	( ) _____	Phone:	( ) _____

73

All persons whose names appear on your title should be included in the seller's space. All persons whose names will appear on the new title shall be listed in the buyer's space using that name in which they desire to take title. This section may additionally ask which city or state each party is currently from.

Date of Agreement - Enter the date your contract is being signed.

Property Address - Enter the complete address of your property that is being sold, including zip code.

Legal Description - Enter the full legal description of your property as stated by the county in which your property is located. This description can be found on your tax bill, grant deed, trust deed, or other legal documents relating to your property.

Purchase Price - State the price of your property that you and your Buyer have agreed upon.

Deposit - Known as good faith or earnest money, this sum of money is received by the seller from the buyer and will accompany the agreement to sell real estate as the property is placed into escrow. The deposit is not to be confused with the down payment, though it eventually becomes part of the same fund. The amount of the deposit is generally an amount that has been determined by the seller or has been negotiated between the seller and buyer. If the deposit amount were to be perceived as a percentage of the sales price, a "normal" sum may vary considerably from as low as one percent to maybe as high as three percent. This sum should be selected carefully, for it acts as a retainer and proves your buyer's intention as you take your property off the market.

Escrow Company - This term may appear in the same sentence as the deposit, for it is asking you to state the name of the escrow company in which the deposit will be placed in trust. if your buyer does not have a preference, the you select an escrow company. If there is another property connected to your sale (the buyer may have sold his previous home, or you may be purchasing a new home, it is often wise to use the same escrow company. That company can then watch both escrows and assure that the escrows either close together or close in a timely manner. If neither your buyer nor yourself have any preference, then look through the yellow pages and find an escrow company which is conveniently located to both you and your buyer.

Your escrow company will help you with all steps following the sales agreement—so relax!

Approximate Principal Balance of First Mortgage, Interest Rate, and Approximate Monthly Payment - State here the loan amount, i.e., the amount your buyer will be borrowing. Use either the amount that was determined on your worksheet or an amount that your buyer requests. State the approximate monthly payment as computed on your worksheet. Note: The final interest rate and monthly payment will probably vary from those in your worksheet. These numbers will not be binding and are for information purposes. If your buyer is assuming your existing loan, then state this loan balance and interest rate.

Remainder of Down Payment - This is the amount remaining after subtracting from the purchase price the loan amount and the deposit.

Total - This is the total value of adding together the loan amount, deposit, and remainder of down payment. This total value will equal the purchase price.

Example:
Purchase Price = $187,900

Method of Payment:

1) Deposit amount to be held in
    trust by ABC Escrow Company $3,000.00
2) Approximate Principal Balance
    or New Loan Amount $162,783.00

    Mortgage Holder   XYZ Savings & Loan

Interest Rate   8 percent per annum

Term of Loan   30 years

3)   Remainder of Down Payment $22,117.00
     (to be furnished at closing)
     Total $187,900.00

» Note: As previously stated, the estimated Closing Costs that YOU determine in your worksheet will NOT be recorded on this contract, as it is NOT an agreement between you and your buyer. The value that you determined to be the closing costs has been deducted from the remainder of down payment.

Remember, we are working backward here. If your buyer said that he had $30,000 to place as a down payment, the closing costs (calculated on the worksheet to be $4,883) were assumed to be part of this $30,000. This way there is less chance of a shortage of funds at the final hour. The true down payment was determined by subtracting $4,883 from $30,000, which is $25,117. Subtract the $3,000 deposit from this figure and you have $22,117 remaining of the down payment.

Example:

$30,000.00	Funds Available
$ (-)$4,883.00	Estimated Closing Costs
= $25,117.00	Total Down Payment
(-)$3,000.00	Deposit
$22,117.00	Remainder of Down

Payment (Paid at Close of Escrow)

Closing Date - Select a date on which this transaction is to be completed. This means that all funds have been transferred, escrow is complete, and the deed and possession have been delivered. NormaL escrow periods will usually last anywhere from thirty days to ninety days, however, you and your buyer must carefully select this date as it affects both of you! You may be relying on the funds from this sale to finance another transaction, and your buyer may be relying on funds from another transaction to fund this one. This is also the date that you and your buyer will be targeting your move.

Included with Purchase - This section allows seller and buyer to record specific personal property or agreements which are to be included in the purchase price of the property. These items would not normally be associated with the transaction of selling real estate. They may have been part of a negotiated agreement that you and your buyer had at the time of the offer. Items that could fall into this category may be furniture (not built-ins), refrigerators, washers and dryers, area rugs, paintings and pictures, or an agreement to replace an item that would be in a state that would otherwise be considered normal wear.

Items that are normally included in the purchase price of real estate would be such things as window shades, curtains and blinds, wall-to-wall carpeting, built-in or attached appliances, light fixtures, plumbing fixtures and hardware, TV antennas, built-in air coolers or air conditioners, mailboxes, garage door openers, and landscaping. These are all items which are attached to the property. They need not be included in this section unless it has been specifically negotiated that a certain item be excluded.

If this is the case, then it should be stated.

Special Clauses or Other Agreements - List any other agreements which may have been reached between you and your buyer. Such special agreements that may be worth mentioning are:

✓ Rent Backs: In the event that the closing date that was selected by you and your buyer does not allow you sufficient time to move, you may want to consider renting the property back from your buyer. This means that after the closing date (your buyer is now legal owner of the property), you may stay in the property for a predetermined length of time and for a predetermined monthly rental fee. The time period and rental fee may be whatever is negotiated between you and your buyer, but it should be stated in this section of the contract.

✓ Contingencies: You and your buyer may have agreed at the time of your offer to sell your property subject to a certain condition. A very common contingency, and one to approach with extreme caution, is the buyer's purchase of your home contingent upon the sale of his home.

This means that if the buyer does not sell his home, then he is not committed to buy your home. Contingencies very often reflect and create uncertainties, and it is our opinion that you, as the success-oriented owner, take all measures to avoid uncertainties!

» Note: Qualifying for a loan is not a contingency and should not be handled as such.

Contingencies very often reflect and create uncertainties, and it is our opinion that you, as the success-oriented owner, take all measures to avoid uncertainties!

✓ Used Home Warranties: It is a good idea, when buying and selling used homes, to attach some form of warranty with the sale. There are companies that offer insurance policies which cover certain basic elements of a used home against malfunction that occurs after the buyer takes possession of the property.

A used-home warranty is often an effective sale tool in clinching a sale.

Policies such as this vary in cost depending on the extent of coverage and the value of the property. An average cost may be in the range of $200 to $400.

This expense is paid through escrow and can be paid by either the buyer or the seller. The policy period generally lasts for one year and may be renewable.

A used-home warranty is often an effective sale tool in clinching a sale. If a buyer is reluctant to purchase your home because of its age, then you can quickly remedy their fears. Offer to provide, at your expense, a used-home warranty.

You can locate a used-home warranty carrier by inquiring at your escrow office. They will be more than happy to give you a recommendation. If a warranty is desired, then it should be stated in this section concerning Special Clauses or Other Agreements.

Commission To Broker: This section will usually appear somewhere toward the end of the agreement and applies to the funds that would have been due to the real estate agency for selling your home. Cross this section out and give yourself a good pat on the back!

The following terms may be found in your agreement and are placed there as clauses or statements which define laws applying to the real estate industry. They are there so that both buyer and seller are aware of such laws as they apply to their agreement.

Prorations - States that any taxes, insurance, interest, rents, or other expenses and income that have not been paid or collected at the time of closing, will be prorated or distributed accordingly between the buyer and seller. Proration is handled through escrow and is usually included in the closing costs.

Clear Title - States that the seller shall convey, or pass to the buyer, a title to the property which is clear or marketable. This means that the title is to be free from liens, assessments, encumbrances, etc. A title may possess varying degrees of "clearness." Therefore, "marketable" would be defined as accepted by a title insurance company or lender. If the title cannot be made marketable, then the seller must refund the deposit to the buyer and cancel the agreement.

Default by Buyer - States that if the buyer fails to perform any of the conditions or requirements placed upon him by this contract, then the seller may retain all funds (the deposit) used in connection with, and as consideration for, the contract. These funds will be used as liquidated damages and will represent the full claim for damages against the buyer. The seller will also be released from his obligation to sell his property to the buyer.

Default of Seller - States that if the seller fails to perform any of the conditions or requirements placed upon him by this contract, the buyer has the right to demand a refund of the money (the deposit) that he has placed in connection with, and as consideration for this contract. The seller would then be released from his obligation to sell his property to the buyer. The buyer has the other option to pursue his right of specific performance, which is to legally pursue his right to purchase the property per the conditions of the contract.

Restrictions, Easements, and Limitations - States that the buyer will be taking title to the property subject to the conditions that currently exist. Such conditions may be zoning restrictions, requirements imposed by the government, restrictions which may apply to your particular sub-development, and easements.

Maintenance - States that between the date of this contract and the date of closing this property shall be maintained by the seller in the same manner and condition as it existed when this contract was signed. This includes the maintenance of all lawns, trees, shrubs, bushes, and pools, as well as all interior maintenance. This does not include the natural aging, or wear and tear, that occurs on the property in that time period.

Termite Inspection - States that the seller agrees to have his property inspected by a state-licensed pest exterminator for live, wood destroying insects, fungus, or wood rot. If such infestation is found, then the seller will agree to have treated and corrected, at his own expense, the infestation and visible structural damage caused as a result. This correction should be complete prior to the close of escrow.

The termite report, which is the result of this inspection, and the costs for correction will usually be billed to the owner through escrow. In the unlikely event the cost was to exceed three percent of the purchase price, then the buyer can elect to pay the difference or forfeit the sales agreement.

___

In the event the roof was in need of repair, the seller's expense will be limited to three percent of the purchase price.
___

Walk-Through Inspection - states that the buyer, or hired agent, has the right to inspect the property in what is known as the walk-through. This inspection should be performed no less than fifteen days before the close of escrow. Its purpose is to determine the working order of such things as appliances, plumbing, air conditioning and heating systems, electrical systems, sprinklers, and pool equipment. The buyer is also entitled to have the roof inspected by a licensed roofing contractor to determine its water-tight condition. The seller shall then pay for repairs as necessary and have such items in working order prior to the close of escrow. Within forty-eight hours before the close of escrow, and after giving notice to the seller, the buyer may re-inspect the property to ensure that the repairs have been made.

In the event the roof was in need of repair, the seller's expense will be limited to three percent of the purchase price. If the cost of these repairs were to exceed three percent, then the buyer can elect to pay the difference or forfeit the sales agreement.

Homeowners' Association - States that if your property belongs to, or provides membership to, a homeowners' association, then the amount of the monthly association dues be disclosed, and that copies of its bylaws and CC&Rs (Covenants, Conditions, and Restrictions) be given to the buyer or the escrow company prior to the close of escrow.

Vested Title - There may be a section in the contract that asks for the manner in which title will be taken by the buyer. This question will also be asked during escrow. It is important that your buyer be prepared and understand this, as the manner in which they take title may have significant legal and tax consequences. For example, if your buyer is single or divorced, then he or she may want to take title as "an unmarried man" (or woman). If your buyer is separated, then he or she may want to take title as "a married man" (or woman) as his or her "sole and separate property." If your buyers are a married couple, and they desire the right to survivorship, then they will most likely want to take title as "joint tenants." If your buyers are not sure, then they should either talk to the people at the escrow office, or consult with an attorney.

And finally, the last section of this agreement will ask for the address, phone number, date, and signature of both the buyer and seller.

While this should take no explaining, filling in these spaces will be the most important feat that you accomplish during your entire campaign. You have now sold your home! Shake your buyers' hands and reassure them of the great value they have just purchased. Let them know how much you have enjoyed the home in the years that you have been there.

You have now sold your home!

CHAPTER VIII

THE ESCROW

You now have a buyer who you feel is qualified to purchase your home. You also have a sales contract with that buyer. The next and final step is to place your property sale into escrow.

Do not lose your momentum at this point. When you hit a home run, you must still run the bases.

You have successfully prepared your home, advertised your home, showed your home, and negotiating the sale of your home. Congratulations! You should be proud of yourself. You will most likely be experiencing an overwhelming sense of accomplishment, and you deserve this. It cannot be stressed enough, however, that you must keep your motivation alive. Do not lose your momentum at this point. When you hit a home run, you must still run the bases. Events have been known to cause a 'good sale' in the beginning to somehow manage to fall through at the eleventh hour. If one were to analyze what happened, it would probably be found that failure occurred because of a lack of communication, a lack of understanding, or the failure to push hard enough. Use these facts to your advantage and stay alert.

The period in which the sale of your home is in escrow is basically a period which is handled by outside agencies: the escrow company, the bank, the title insurance company, etc. Your participation in the escrow process will be limited. Your involvement, however, may make all the difference in the world to assure a smooth escrow. Be available, and be flexible.

In very general terms, an escrow can be defined as some form of an agreement which is trusted to, and held in the hands, of a third party and delivered after certain acts or specific requirements have been met.

It is best that you both visit the escrow company at the same time.

An escrow, as it applies to real estate, can be described in the following manner: when the interest in real estate is transferred from one party to another, a good number of documents have to be drawn up and facts and legal matters have to be checked and cleared. Finances have to be arranged and banks consulted. Companies that specialize in the gathering of such facts are known as escrow companies. They hold the agreement that you have made with your buyer until such time that all the facts have been cleared and conditions of the agreement have been met. They are then paid for their efforts by both buyer and seller. In some states, real estate attorneys are used instead of escrow companies. They provide the same function, however, as the escrow companies.

It is time for you and your buyer to make some plans. You need to place your property into escrow, and your buyer needs to make some major financial arrangements. Unless they are paying cash for your home, this means that they must apply and qualify for a loan.

Make arrangements with your buyer, before they leave your home if possible, to visit the escrow company that you both have selected. It is best that you both visit the escrow company at the same time. This way you both can present your agreement to escrow, and if there are any questions regarding certain facts, they can be answered by either one or both of you. You simply will know where each other stands. Your first visit to your escrow company will probably be very brief. This may be the only visit needed until final papers are ready to be signed. Near the beginning of the escrow, you and your buyer will be receiving escrow instructions. These instructions will primarily consist of an extended format of the agreement that you have provided to escrow. Additional questions may be asked and statements made which apply specifically to your housing development or county. Read the instructions very carefully, as they reflect conditions that your buyer and yourself have agreed to. The terminology, for the most part, will be familiar to you, as it has been derived from the statements and facts taken from the agreement you and your buyer have signed. You will be signing the escrow instructions and returning them to the escrow company. It may be pointed out here, that if you and your buyer have requested a very short escrow and have a limited amount of time, then you can hand deliver, for yourself and your buyer, all documents that would ordinarily be sent through the mail. This will help to greatly expedite matters.

Of utmost importance during your escrow will be the formal qualifying of your buyer to gain a bank loan for your property. You have already prequalified him, and you feel reasonably safe. It is now up to the bank to do the same.

Have your buyer make contact with the loan representative that you contacted. This representative will help your buyer with any further questions and help him with the application.

By the time you signed the sales agreement with your buyer, you probably had developed a good feel for the financial direction your buyer was headed. You knew how much he needed to borrow and maybe which bank he wanted to borrow from. You did your homework early and talked to a bank on your own. You were given a few loan applications and were given basic insight as to the loan programs this bank had to offer. If your buyer, at this point, is not clear on his direction, then you need to help him. Give him one of the loan applications that you received and refresh him on the basic programs your bank is offering. This information can be taken directly from the loan flier that you received with the applications. Have your buyer make contact with the loan representative that you contacted. This representative will help your buyer with any further questions and help him with the application. You should call this representative a few days later and find out how the first meeting went. He can also tell you how the prequalification process looks. It will take anywhere from one to three weeks for the bank to formally qualify your buyer. Tell the loan representative that if you can be of any help to him to let you know. You have the right to know the status of your buyer, so do not hesitate to maintain communication lines.

Over the next few weeks you will continue to receive paperwork to be reviewed, signed, and returned. You will receive such documents as the Property Transfer Information Sheet, which asks for general information about your property and its existing loans (loan numbers, loan balance, etc.). You will receive the IRS taxpayer information sheet, which asks for the address and selling price of the property. It also asks for your Social Security number and/or status of citizenship. You will receive a Real Estate Transfer Disclosure Statement, which asks for you to identify the features and equipment that your home contains. It will ask you to verify that the equipment is in working condition. You will most likely be receiving: Amendments to Escrow Instructions, which merely corrects discrepancies as they are discovered and restates conditions as they change throughout the escrow period. You may also receive various documents that relate specifically to your particular housing development or to your county.

Over the next few weeks you will continue to receive paperwork to be reviewed, signed, and returned.

During this time, a title search will be performed on your property. As properties are owned, and sometimes even after they are sold and resold, evidence of the title remaining clear, or faultless, may diminish.

Such things as liens (the attachment of a debt to a property) and assessments may have gone unsatisfied. The buyer has the legal right to take possession of the property completely free from such risks associated with flaws in the title. A title company is therefore hired, usually by the escrow company, to perform a title search. The title company will research public records and present a history of the title of the property. Based on this research, the title company will issue an insurance policy which will either guarantee a clear title or will guarantee a clear title with noted exceptions. In either case, the insurance policy will guarantee the title to be risk-free and will be paid for by the seller, through escrow. Your buyer will be furnished, during the escrow, a Preliminary Title Report for inspection. He has the right to disapprove any exceptions that were found. You, as the seller, must clear up these exceptions prior to the close of escrow.

In either case, however, the bank will schedule and perform an appraisal.

In order for the bank to determine how much money can be loaned to your buyer, it must determine what it considers to be the true market value of your home. This is accomplished by means of a bank appraisal. Determining the market value is very important to a lending institution providing funds for a property. This market value is required to determine the loan-to-value ratio. As discussed earlier, the loan-to-value ratio represents the proportion of funds which are borrowed to the total value, or market value, of the property. The bank maintains different parameters for loans based on the different values of this ratio. If the loan-to-value ratio is too high, the bank may not issue the loan at all. If your buyer is providing a large down payment, then the loan-to-value ratio will be lower and will not be a critical issue in the loan qualification process. In either case, however, the bank will schedule and perform an appraisal.

You will receive a call from an appraiser hired by the bank or lending institution of your buyer to make an appointment with you to meet at your home.

He will measure the square footage of your home and will evaluate your home's overall condition. He will also make note of upgrades that are present. It may be helpful to your appraiser if you point out specific upgrades or custom features which he may not have noticed, particularly features which other homes (comparables) in your neighborhood may not have. It will most always be to your benefit that the appraised value result, if not at the purchase price, at the highest value possible.

As escrow progresses, and as forms and information are sent back and forth, it is strongly recommended that you make contact with the agent who is working directly with your escrow. Ask how things are progressing and if any problems have occurred. Ask if they have received word from the bank on the formal qualification of your buyer. Find out exactly where your escrow stands. The sooner you find out about a possible problem, the more prepared you will be to assist in correcting it, and the more time will be saved.

It is not uncommon for little problems to pop up during and throughout a perfectly good escrow. It should even be expected. Each little problem will have a solution. It is also possible for escrows to exist which seem to be plagued with bigger problems. Do not become discouraged, as every problem has some form of solution. The escrow company is used to dealing with these types of problems and will usually make every effort to solve them. This is part of their function. There may be times, however, when your participation can make a significant impact on the progress and even the success of your escrow.

Problem Escrows - And What You Can Do

BUYER DOES NOT QUALIFY FOR LOAN:
1) Loan-to-value ratio Is Too High - loan amount has to come down and down payment amount must increase. Buyer must come up with extra cash for the down payment. Talk to them and find out if other sources of cash are available: loan from a family member, cash from savings bonds or treasury bills, etc. You may lower your purchase price slightly, enough to allow your buyer to qualify. You may also accomplish this by offering to pay your buyer's closing costs. It may be just enough to make the difference.

2) Buyer's Debt Ratio Is Too High - Buyer's monthly payment must decrease. This can be accomplished by decreasing the loan amount or changing the loan pro-gram (changing from a fixed-rate loan to an adjustable-rate loan to lower the interest rate, etc.). You may adjust your price slightly or pay the buyer's closing costs. This will also result in a decreased loan amount and may be just enough to push your buyer over the edge. Other factors will contribute to your buyer's debt ratio, such as increases in income and the amount of other monthly payments. These may be difficult to change, however,

within a short period of time. He may, though, have a car payment or some payment which is near the end of its term. It is not uncommon for accounts like these to be paid off through escrow by the buyer for the purpose of qualifying.

For example, if your property taxes are not currently paid, or if you have missed any payment in the years you have owned your home, a lien may have been filed against your property.

---

3) Buyer's Credit Rating Is Not Sufficient - The bank may ask your buyer for a letter explaining marks against his credit. This will give your buyer a chance to offer explanations. If the bank does not request this letter, then ask the bank if one can be provided to help your buyer.

4) When you originally worked with your buyer, you created a worksheet. This worksheet created such ratios as the ones discussed above. If these ratios were within, or even close to the safe working ranges, then some bank, whether it be the one you are working with or any other bank, will qualify your buyer. It is a matter of finding this bank and working with it. You may be quite surprised how different each bank regards qualifications. Some banks simply may not want to lend money. There will be the right bank to meet your buyer's and your needs.

LIENS OR ASSESSMENTS ARE DISCOVERED BY YOUR TITLE SEARCH:

If a lien or an assessment is discovered to be attached to your property, it is extremely important that it be cleared up as quickly as possible. A lien is a record that has been filed by another party which claims an interest in your property to satisfy and unpaid debt.

For example, if your property taxes are not currently paid, or if you have missed any payment in the years you have owned your home, a lien may have been filed against your property. You will now have to pay these taxes or make arrangements to have them paid through escrow. Likewise, an assessment is the valuation of your property for the specific purpose of creating a tax. A special assessment will exist when your property is taxed for a specific purpose. If these assessments go unpaid, then just as a lien, they will be attached to your property and will prevent you from selling the property until the debt is paid. If these exist, then clear them up, as they will only create delays in your escrow.

SALE OF BUYER'S PROPERTY BECOMES DELAYED:

You, as a For Sale By Owner, have had maximum control over the sale of your home. Your buyer may be counting on the funds from the sale of his home to purchase your property. You will not have the same control over his sale as you have had with yours. In the event that there is a delay with your buyer's sale, then you must remain patient and flexible. If the escrow company that you are using is handling both escrows as recommended, then you may have immediate access to information about the delay. A compromise between all three parties may become necessary to resolve and avoid any further delay. An adjustment in your escrow closing date may be the result of your compromise and should be considered a battle won in your efforts to assure a successful escrow.

A secondary function of the walk-through will be to familiarize your buyer with the operating functions of your home.

As you approach your closing date, it will become time for you to tie up the loose ends that remain. It will be a good idea for you to read over your sales agreement and your escrow instructions. Doing this will refresh your memory as to any special agreements that may have been made with your buyer. Did you agree to paint the attic or were you going to change the chandelier? It will also refresh your memory on other basic matters that may need your attention. If your property belongs to a homeowners' association, have you furnished the escrow company or the buyer with the CC&Rs? Have you arranged for your termite inspection?

The termite inspection, in most cases, will be your responsibility and should be taken care of in sufficient time (fifteen days or more) before the close of escrow. This will allow time for corrective work to be performed if required. If you are in doubt where to find a licensed pest exterminator, simply look in the yellow pages under pest control services. Your escrow company can also provide you with recommended exterminators.

You and your buyer will be scheduling a convenient time for a walk-through. Again, you should, schedule this at least fifteen days before the close of escrow to allow sufficient time for any needed repairs. Your walk-through will be somewhat less formal than if it had been conducted through a real estate agency, though its function shall be the same. Its purpose will be to determine the working condition of appliances, plumbing fixtures, air conditioning and heating systems, electrical systems, sprinklers, etc.

A secondary function of the walk-through will be to familiarize your buyer with the operating functions of your home. This will be your chance to show your buyer how the sprinkling system operates, how the heater is turned on, and so forth. If you own a pool, be sure to go over its operation in some detail. After the walk-through is complete, the buyer has the right to come back once more to verify that repairs which may have been needed were made.

THE CLOSE OF ESCROW

The close of escrow, otherwise known as the closing, is that time when the final funds are transferred and the deed on your property is recorded. This is the time that legal possession occurs and your buyer becomes the true owner of the property.

All of the agreements made with your buyer have been met, all inspections have been performed, and finances have been arranged.

You will receive at closing, or shortly thereafter, a closing, or Settlement Statement.

You will be asked, just prior to closing, to make one final trip to the escrow company. You will sign a grant deed, or equivalent transfer document, and any remaining documents which relate to the transfer. Your signature will be notarized, and the deed will be recorded in the county that your property is situated. This recording is done by your county recorder and marks the official closing of your property. Your home is now formally sold.

You will receive at closing, or shortly thereafter, a closing, or Settlement Statement. This Settlement Statement represents a final accounting of the entire transaction and will consist of all fees that were charged including escrow fees, reconveyance fees, title fees, and so on. This statement will include all prorated interest and taxes that have been charged, loan payoffs that have been made, and refunds due. Overall, this statement consists of a complete list of debits, or charges, made to your account and credits made to your account. The debits will be added to the credits and the result will be the balance due you. You will receive with this settlement statement check made out to you.

The check that you now have in your hands represents the equity that you had in your home, or the part of your home, in dollars, that totally belonged to you. This number was $10,000, $20,000, or $30,000 higher, maybe even more, because you chose to sell your home yourself.

You have faced your challenge. You have experienced success. Now, go out and treat yourself!

The check that you now have in your hands represents the equity that you had in your home...

CHAPTER IX

IN CLOSING

Let's travel back in time for a few minutes, back when you were, let's say, in junior high school. You were in a classroom in which your teacher has just assigned to the class a term report. This term report seemed to you like the most inconceivable, difficult chore that you could ever set out to accomplish. Worse yet, you had no idea in the world where to begin and what to write your report about. You experienced early in life that emotion that we discussed previously, fear. You were experiencing the fear of the unknown and most likely the fear of failure. Unlike your adult life, however, in school you knew you had to start and complete your report or you stood a good chance of failing the course. What you inevitably learned through this was that first, you were motivated by your desire to pass the course. You then learned that once you selected a subject for your report, and the minute you placed your pencil on the paper, you were already halfway done.

Too many of us today, after the schooling is long past, fail to remember or take the time to create our own new challenges. There is no one assigning us classroom reports that we have to complete. Since we are not pushed by anyone but ourselves, it often seems easier to let somebody else do it, or to simply allow a challenge to slip past.

Do you remember how you felt when you finally completed your report? You had conquered that inconceivable challenge and most likely felt as though you were on top of the world. Even if that report didn't come in at the top of the class, you knew you had met the challenge. The memory and the satisfaction created from that success will far outlast that battering fear of failure.

You, as a homeowner, have been inspired and have been motivated to meet a challenge, that of selling your own home. Your motivation has been derived from many sources: your desire to earn yourself thousands of dollars, your desire to maintain control, your desire to accomplish, and most likely your desire to experience a little esteem from success.

Your decision to sell your own home is like the subject of your report.

You have chosen a goal and given it direction. You are already halfway there! Having read this complete book, you now have the material that will really make it happen, step by step, from start to finish. All that's left is the application of knowledge gained—your key to success. Just remember the thrill that you will receive, and the true satisfaction that will be yours to keep, when you hand to your buyer the key!

If you have any questions regarding the information presented in this book, or regarding particular circumstances that you may encounter in the sale of your home, you may write to the author. Please send your request and a self-addressed, stamped envelope to:

Inquiry
14252 Culver Drive, Suite A122
Irvine, CA 92714

QUICK-REFERENCE GLOSSARY

adjustable-rate mortgage - A loan program in which the interest rate is allowed to float or vary, in parallel with the interest rate of a stated published index.

agent - A person who has the authority to act for another. In the sense of this book, any person professionally associated with the real estate industry.

amortization - The process of breaking down a loan or a debt into a series of equal payments. The payments will include both the principal amount and the interest amount specified in the loan.

appraisal - An estimate of the value of a piece of real estate.

appraiser - A person who specializes in estimating the value of real estate.

assessment - The valuation of a piece of real estate for the specific purpose of creating a tax.

broker - A person who has been authorized to represent another, who negotiates for the sale, management, or lease of real estate in exchange for a commission.

caravan - As it applies to real estate, a term used to describe the specific day and the process of holding open houses at new homes that have been listed. These open houses are held by professionals in the real estate industry for the purpose of being previewed by other professionals in the industry.

CC&Rs - Covenants, conditions, and restrictions that relate to property owners how have membership in a homeowners' association. These are all of the laws, rules, and regulations which govern the members of the homeowners' association.

closing costs - All of the costs or charges associated with the transfer of real estate.

closing date - The day of a real estate transaction that the deed is recorded and the buyer takes legal possession of the property.

closing statement - A list of debits and credits which represent the final accounting of an entire real estate transaction.

consideration - Anything of value given in exchange for entering into a contract.

contingency - Any agreement which is dependent on another condition to take place. If the other condition does not occur, then the agreement does not exist and cannot be enforced.

debt ratio - The proportion of a loan applicant's monthly income which is used to pay major debts. This ratio is created by dividing the value for the major debt monthly expense by the gross monthly income.

deed - A document or record which conveys the title to a piece of real estate.

grant deed - The deed that the seller conveys and warrants to the buyer that he has not previously passed title.

trust deed - A document which serves as evidence that the buyer of a piece of real estate will pledge this real estate as security for a debt. The trust deed will be dissolved at such time as the debt is paid.

default - Failure to fulfill a promise as defined in a contract.

deposit - A sum of money or other consideration which is presented in connection with an offer to purchase real estate.

depreciation - Loss in value as a result of any cause.

easement - The right of a party to make limited use of a piece of real estate which is owned by another.

equity - The monetary value which reflects the owner's exclusive interest in a piece of real estate; that portion which is separate from all loans and debts and belongs completely to the owner.

escrow company - A company which specializes in the gathering and organization of facts and the initiation of documents which are necessary for the successful transfer of real estate.

finder's fee - An amount of money or other form of consideration which is offered to a second party for his efforts in bringing a buyer for property being sold by the first party.

fixed-rate mortgage - A loan program in which the interest rate remains fixed or stationary throughout the life of the loan.

Foreclosure - The legal steps that need to be taken by the holder of a mortgage, when a debt is in default, before proceedings can take place against the property to satisfy that debt.

FSBO - For Sale By Owner, or a party that chooses to sell, on their own, their home or other property owned by them, exclusive of real estate agencies.

gross monthly income - The total income earned on a monthly basis before taxes and deductions are included. If two or more people are applying for a loan together, then the gross monthly income will include combined incomes.

interest - The percentage of a sum of money which is earned by a bank or lending institution in exchange for lending that money.

joint tenancy - A joint estate in which two or more people hold equal ownership in the same property, and includes the right of survivorship; if one owner dies, his interest passes to the remaining owner

legal description - A means of identifying and describing the exact boundaries of a parcel of land and is created by various survey systems. This is the description on record in the county in which the property is situated.

lien - A record filed against an owner's property, by another party, which claims an interest in that property to satisfy a debt. A lien may cause a property to be sold or prevent the property from being sold until the debt is satisfied.

liquidated damages - A fixed sum of money agreed upon between parties of a contract, and not to be exceeded, which represents the complete claim for damages against the party who breaches the contract.

listing price - This term specifically refers to a property that has been listed with a real estate agency, and refers to the price at which the property is being offered. The listing price is the same as the asking price and may differ from the selling price.

loan assumption - The act and the ability of the buyer in a real estate transaction to assume and take over the existing loan obligations of the seller.

loan-to-value ratio - The percentage and proportion of the market value of a piece of real estate which is paid for with borrowed money. This ratio represents the bank or lender's interest in the property.

model home - A home which is used as a display for the purpose of selling other homes.

mortgage - The instrument or record which represents the evidence that real estate has been pledged as security for a debt.

mortgagee - The bank, creditor, or lender under a mortgage.

mortgagor - The borrower or debtor under a mortgage.

notarize - To represent as being authentic by means of a person licensed as a notary public acting as a witness.

offer - The presentation of a request to purchase real estate, at a given price, with hopes of acceptance. When an offer is presented by a real estate agency, it is accompanied by a deposit of earnest money.

open house - A home which has been opened and made accessible to potential purchasers for their inspection, without the need for an appointment.

principal - The actual amount of a debt or loan balance not including the interest. Also, a principal is a person who is represented by an agent; the client.

proration - To distribute proportionally or accordingly the debits and credits of an account.

qualify - The ability of a buyer, or a person applying for a loan, to successfully meet the requirements that have been asked of him as a condition for granting the loan.

realtor - A broker who is a member of a local real estate board and is associated with the National Association of Real Estate Boards. In the sense of this book, realtor is used as a general term to define any salesperson, agent, or broker associated with the real estate industry.

reconveyance fee - The charge associated with the transfer of title of a piece of real estate from one party to the next.

rent back - A prearranged agreement between the seller of a property and the buyer whereas, after the close of escrow and the buyer becomes owner of the property, the seller can remain in the property and pay rent to the buyer for a stated period of time.

single party listing - An agreement between the owner of a piece of real estate and a real estate agency whereas the owner's property becomes listed with that agency only in the event that a buyer is brought to owner by the agency. The agreement will specify terms that both the owner and the agency have negotiated.

specific performance - The legal requirement that a party to a real estate contract carry out all terms agreed to in that contract, in lieu of damages paid.

title - The recorded proof or evidence of ownership rights of a piece of real estate.

title search - A study of the history of the title to a given property to determine if it is free from defects.

vested title - The right of ownership and the privileges associated with such ownership. The manner in which the title is taken or vested will have consequences over such privileges of ownership.

walk through - The right of the buyer of a property to inspect, or have inspected, its functioning condition prior to taking possession.

APPENDICES

ITEMS THAT YOU WILL NEED

2 For Sale signs

1 Open House sign

1 Mortgage Payment Tables guide

3 Loan Applications from local bank

3 Loan Program Fliers from a local bank

3 Real Estate Sales Agreement contract forms

1 Pad of paper 8 1/2" x 11"

OPTIONAL ITEMS

✓ Flags for Open House

✓ Arrow directional signs for Open House

✓ Business/finance calculator

** WESTVIEW PROMENADE **
by J.P. Brooks
12345 Pine Lane, Irvine

Offered is plan 260; 3 bedrooms, 2 1/2 baths + family room, 1950 sq.ft. Home is situated on a private driveway in a very private setting. Probably the most complete and custom landscaped unit to be found! Home is absolutely ready to provide a carefree California lifestyle!

INTERIOR

* Rare covered exterior entry
* Hardwood oak entry and family room floors
* Mirrored dining room wall, ceiling to floor, side to side
* Mirrored wardrobe closet doors
* Built-in trash compactor
* Built-in microwave oven
* Custom wooden blinds throughout with matching custom draperies
* Plantation shutters between living room and family room
* Heavy duty shelving in garage
* Upgraded neutral color carpet
* Fire protection system throughout home, including automatic fire alarm
* Forced air conditioning and heating
* Garage door opener

EXTERIOR

* Completely landscaped in a lush tropical setting including, palm trees, banana trees, and never-ending flower gardens.
* Two raised concrete decks (wired for fountains) with brick trim and inlay and matching walkways all lavishly covered with outdoor carpeting.
* Automatic sprinklers, front and rear, for worry-free maintenance.
* Automatic lighting systems in front, side, and rear yards.

Association pools, spas, and recreational parks available to all Westview residents.

This breathtaking home is being offered at $329,900.

Evenings and weekends PH (123) 765-4321
Weekdays   PH (765) 123-4567 Ext. 000

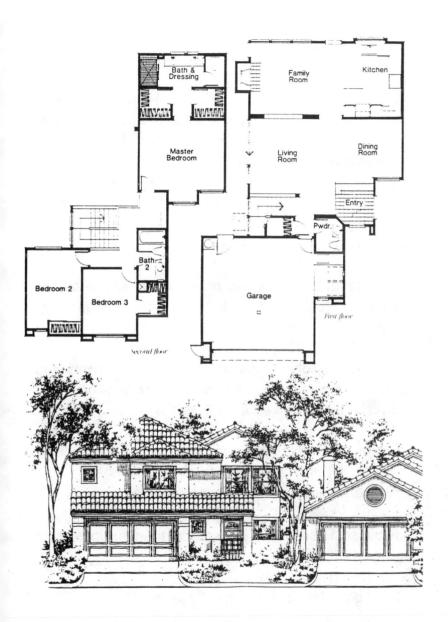

Bath & Dressing

Kitchen

Family Room

Master Bedroom

Living Room

Dining Room

Entry

Pwdr.

Bath 2

Bedroom 2

Bedroom 3

Garage

First floor

Second floor

CHECKLIST ✍️

☐ Green lawn - make sure your lawn is the greenest in the neighborhood. Visit the local hardware store or garden shop. Invest in a good quality lawn food (to make your lawn healthy) and ammonia sulfate (to quickly bring out the green).

☐Keep your lawn mowed and edged - more so than normal.

☐Locate and remove all dead or unhealthy-looking plants. If you can't afford to replace them, then leave them out.

☐Add some color. - Invest in a few potted plants and place them by the door step or strategic locations. You can take these with you.

☐Prune and trim all trees and bushes.

☐Broken windows - they must be replaced.

☐Roof shingles or tiles - are any of them mislocated or hanging off the edge of the roof?

☐Mail box - has it been recently painted?

☐Draperies and window blinds - how do they look from the outside? Which position do they look best in? Are they hanging straight?

☐Doorbell - does it work?

☐Front door - access is first gained through this door. Is it clean? If it is in need of paint, then it should be painted. Even if your entire house is in need of paint (and you can't afford to spend the money at this time), it will make a far better first impression if you paint the front door.

☐Carpets - they may or may not be in the best condition, but make sure they are clean. Even a decorator's delight with dirty carpets can be a turnoff.

☐Walls - must also be clean and free from holes and dents. If need be, use spackling compound for the dents and holes and do a little touch-up painting.

☐Floors - clean and waxed.

☐Kitchen and Bathroom - a key tattletailer to the condition and maintenance background of your home will be found in the kitchen and bathrooms.

☐ Grease and dirt around stove and oven?

☐ Is oven clean inside?

❏ Place new burner plates under the burners of your stove if applicable. No matter what condition your old ones are in, new ones will always look better. They are inexpensive and found in most supermarkets.

❏ Clean grouting between tiles around sinks and bathtubs.

❏ Condition of seal around sinks and bathtubs. Does it need cleaning or repair?

❏ Chipped porcelain in sinks and bathtubs. Repair with a porcelain repair product found in your local hardware store.

❏ Faucets and faucet handles - make sure they're clean and sparkling.

❏ Kitchen and bathroom cabinets - in reasonable order.

❏ Burned out light bulbs in fixtures and lamps - replace.

❏ Clean windows - makes everything outside look cleaner.

❏ Backyard - maintain same as front yard - green cut lawn, trimmed bushes and trees, etc.

☐Pool - if you own a pool, keep it clean and clear. A pool is a large investment and a selling feature of your house. It should look inviting.

Real Estate Sales Agreement
(Sample)

I (We) _____ hereinafter referred to as "Seller"

of _____ County and State hereby enter into an agreement with:

_____ hereinafter referred to as "Buyer"

of _____ County and State on this ____ day of _____ 19 ____.

1. I agree to sell my property located at:

   _____
   Street Address

   _____
   City

   _____
   State, Zip Code

   to the Buyer based on conditions set forth in this contract.

2. The legal description of my property is as follows:

   _____
   _____
   _____

3. Buyer agrees to pay the Purchase Price of $_____ and the method of payment shall be:

   a)   Deposit to be held in Trust by _____ in the amount of: $_____

   b)   Approximate Principal Balance on New Loan Amount: $_____
        Mortgage Holder: _____
        Interest Rate: _____
        Term of Loan: _____

   c)   Remainder of Down Payment to be in the amount of: $_____
        or that amount which is required to complete the
        purchase price at Closing.

                                                        Total $_____

4. This contract shall provide for a Closing on or before _____, 19 ____.

5. Buyer and Seller agree that all attached fixtures and fittings including window shades, curtains and blinds, wall to wall carpeting, built-in or attached appliances, lighting fixtures, plumbing fixtures and hardware, TV antennas, built-in air cooler and air conditioners, garage door openers, and landscaping are INCLUDED in the sale of this property. No personal property shall be included unless specifically listed here.

   INCLUDED WITH PURCHASE:

   _____
   _____
   _____

6. No other special agreements between Buyer and Seller shall be binding unless stated here.

   SPECIAL CLAUSES OR AGREEMENTS:

   _____
   _____
   _____

Real Estate Sales Agreement

Pursuant to this agreement, standard real estate laws will apply and include, but not be limited to the following:

7. Prorations: Buyer and Seller understand that all charges and revenues that accrue against the property and not yet paid or collected shall be prorated at the time of Closing between the accounts of the Buyer and Seller.

8. Clear Title: Buyer and Seller understand that Seller shall convey to Buyer a clear or marketable title to said property. If such marketable title cannot be obtained, as would be acceptable to a title insurance company or lender, then Seller shall refund to Buyer the Deposit or any consideration placed in connection with this agreement, and contract will be cancelled.

9. Default of Buyer: Buyer and Seller understand that if Buyer fails to perform any conditions of this contract, then Seller may retain the Deposit, or any consideration placed in connection with this contract, as liquidated damages. This agreement will then be cancelled.

10. Default of Seller: Buyer and Seller understand that if Seller fails to perform any conditions of this contract, then Buyer may elect to demand a full refund of the Deposit or any consideration used in connection with this contract, or demand his right to specific performance.

11. Restrictions, Easements, and Limitations: Buyer and Seller understand that Buyer shall take title to said property subject to all Restrictions, Easements, and Limitations that are currently in force.

12. Maintenance: Buyer and Seller understand that Seller shall maintain said property as it currently exists between this date and the date of Closing. Seller is not responsible for the normal result of aging during this time period.

13. Termite Inspection: Buyer and Seller understand that Seller agrees to have premises inspected by a State Licensed Pest Exterminator for live, wood destroying insects, fungus, or wood rot. If such infestation is found, then Seller shall have treated and any visual structural damage repaired. Seller shall be limited to 3% of the purchase price for repairs. If such costs exceed 3%, then the Buyer can elect to pay the difference or forfeit this contract.

14. Walk-Through Inspection: Buyer and Seller agree that Buyer, or his agent, has the right to inspect premises at least 15 days before Closing to determine the working condition of appliances, plumbing, air conditioning and heating system, electrical systems, sprinklers, pool equipment, and roofing. Seller shall pay for repairs as necessary to bring such items into working condition. Buyer has the right to reinspect premises within 48 hours of Closing to assure that repairs have been made. If roofing repairs are required to achieve a watertight condition, then Seller shall be limited to 3% of the purchase price for such repairs. If costs exceed 3%, the Buyer can elect to pay the difference or forfeit this contract.

15. Homeowner's Association: If the property in this transaction belongs to or provides membership in a Homeowner's Association, then copies of its Bylaws and CC&Rs are to be delivered to the Buyer or the above-stated Escrow Company before Closing. The monthly association dues are: $_____.

16. Unless otherwise stated in the Escrow Instructions, title shall vest as follows:_____

Seller(s): _____   Buyer(s): _____

Dated: _____   Dated: _____
Address: _____   Address: _____

Phone: ( )_____   Phone: ( )_____

PROPERTY	UNIQUE FEATURE	POOL	BED-ROOMS	BATHS	DEN	FAMILY ROOM	DINING ROOM	SIZE (SQ.FT.)	ASKING PRICE	SELLING PRICE

YOUR PROPERTY										

Market Analysis

126

PROPERTY	UNIQUE FEATURE	POOL	BED-ROOMS	BATHS	DEN	FAMILY ROOM	DINING ROOM	SIZE (SQ. FT.)	ASKING PRICE	SELLING PRICE

YOUR PROPERTY										

Market Analysis

INDEX

Accept, Acceptance, Accepted, 52, 69, 82, 113

Access, Accessible, 3, 4, 14, 27, 28, 61, 98, 113

Accompanied, Accompany,11, 37, 52, 74, 113

Accomplish, Accomplished, Accomplishment, 86, 87, 93, 95, 103, 104

Account, Accounting, 100, 101, 108, 113

Accounts, 96

Accuracy, Accurate, 7, 58

Acquired, Acquire, 36, 65, 71

Actual, 3, 26, 59, 64, 113

Actually, 55, 56

Ad, 6, 19, 20, 22, 23, 25, 26, 27, 28, 44, 48, 49

Adjustable, Adjustable-Rate, 56, 57, 61, 62, 66, 67, 68, 95, 107

Advertised, Advertise, Advertisement, Advertising, 11, 19, 20, 26, 27, 35, 87

Aesthetically, 19

Afford, 12, 13, 14, 26, 69

Agency, Agencies, 9, 11, 36, 39, 40, 42, 43, 51, 52, 82, 88, 99, 110, 112, 113, 114

Agent, 52, 84, 94, 107, 113

Agreement, Agreements, 39, 54, 55, 59, 71, 74, 75, 77, 78, 79, 81, 82, 84, 85, 86, 88, 89, 90, 98, 100, 109, 114

Amendments, 92

Amortization, 107

Amount, 18, 35, 38, 43, 49, 51, 52, 57, 58, 59, 60, 61, 62, 63, 67, 70, 74, 75, 76, 85, 90, 95, 107, 110, 113

Analysis, 6, 7

Analyze, 87

Annum, 77

Application, Applications, 55, 90, 91, 104

NOTES

NOTES

NOTES

CONSUMER BOOKS

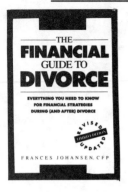

THE FINANCIAL GUIDE TO DIVORCE
How much will a divorce cost? How long will it take?
What do you have? What will you get? Evaluating assets.
(ISBN:0-929230-05-1 United Resource Press/Johansen)

THE CONSUMER GUIDE TO CREDIT
Methods of legally repairing your credit. How to get loans.
Understanding credit reports.
(ISBN:0-929230-06-X United Resource Press/Brown)

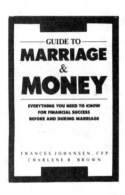

GUIDE TO MARRIAGE & MONEY
Evaluate and plan for: continuing education,
children, home buying, children's education, retirement.
Discussion on understanding basic finance.
(ISBN:0-929230-11-6 United Resource Press/Johansen/Brown)

GUIDE TO SELLING YOUR HOME
Everything you need to know to sell your real estate
without (or with) a broker in a competitive market.
(ISBN:0-929230-07-8 United Resource Press/Greer)

PLEASE BUY/ORDER THROUGH YOUR FAVORITE BOOKSTORE.
{PGW/Ingram}.
LIBRARIES may order through Quality Books (708) 295-1556.
If neither of these options is available to you, you may order through United Resource by
sending a $8.95 Money Order ($5.95/Book + $3.00 shipping and handling)
to: United Resource Press, 4521 Campus, #388, Irvine, CA 92715.

**To receive our Consumer Finance News Update FREE
send Name and Address to:** *Consumer Update,*
4521 Campus, #388 Irvine, CA 92715